LEARNING TO SAFELY SWIM IN THE DEEP END OF THE *FINANCIAL* POOL

CARL F. FELDMAN
FELDMAN FINANCIAL SERVICES, LLC

This book discusses general concepts for retirement planning and is not intended to provide tax or legal advice. Individuals are urged to consult with their tax and legal professionals regarding these issues. It is important to know a) that annuities and some of their features have costs associated with them; b) that annuities used to fund IRAs do not afford any additional measure of tax deferral for the IRA owner; c) that income received from annuities and securities may be taxable; and d) that securities' past performance does not influence or predict future results.

Copyright © 2023 by Gradient Positioning Systems, LLC. All rights reserved. No part of this publication may be reproduced, distributed, or transmitted in any form or by any means, electronic or mechanical, including photocopying, recording, or by any information storage and retrieval system, without written permission of the publisher, except in the case of brief quotations embodied in critical reviews and certain other noncommercial uses permitted by copyright law.

Printed in the United States of America

First Printing, 2023

Gradient Positioning Systems, LLC
4105 Lexington Avenue North, Suite 110
Arden Hills, MN 55126
(877) 901-0894

Contributors: Gradient Positioning Systems, LLC.

Advisory services are offered through Feldman Financial Services, LLC, a Registered Investment Advisor in the State of New Jersey. Insurance products and services are offered through Carl Feldman. Feldman Financial Services, LLC and Carl Feldman are not affiliated with or endorsed by the Social Security Administration or any government agency.

TABLE OF CONTENTS

INTRODUCTION 1

CHAPTER 1: *WHY PLAY IT SAFE?* 7

CHAPTER 2: *WHAT RISK MEANS FOR YOUR FUTURE* 17

CHAPTER 3: *ADDING UP YOUR ASSETS* 25

CHAPTER 4: *INCOME STRATEGY* 31

CHAPTER 5: *UNDERSTANDING SOCIAL SECURITY* 41

CHAPTER 6: *PAYING YOUR FAIR SHARE OF TAXES* 47

CHAPTER 7: *INSURING YOURSELF AGAINST SURPRISES* 57

CHAPTER 8: *EMPOWERING WOMEN AND INDIVIDUALS* 63

CHAPTER 9: *PROTECTING YOUR LEGACY* 67

CHAPTER 10: *TURNING IT INTO A PLAN* 75

CHAPTER 11: *FIND A QUALIFIED FINANCIAL SERVICES PROFESSIONAL* 85

CHAPTER 12: *WHAT'S NEXT?* 95

THANK YOU 105

ABOUT THE AUTHOR 107

INTRODUCTION

Retirement planning is like packing your bags to visit a place you've never been before, on a journey that you don't know how long it will take. There are many ways to plan a retirement, but most people don't know how to do it, because they've never been retired until they suddenly are.

You also only get one shot to do it. A squirrel who saves up its nuts for the winter doesn't get another chance to collect more nuts if it run out—the season is over. Squirrels who choose a cozy and safe nest that's free from danger get to enjoy those nuts all winter long and live a happy and comfortable life.

Retirement has changed drastically since its inception. Where once there were company pensions that took care of you and your spouse as long as you needed them, this has become quite rare these days. Health care has improved drastically and increased the average life span, which is fantastic news for humanity. But it also means that you need to stretch retirement savings a lot longer than you had to 50 years ago.

To put it succinctly, costs and expenses have gone up, while inflation has increased the price of many things, some benefits like pensions appear to be on the decline, and the duration you need savings for has been extended.

Despite these challenges, you can still come up with a retirement plan that works for you and your family. This book contains, what I believe, are the essential retirement-planning strategies that you must know to navigate your retirement with ease. One of the greatest feelings you can have throughout your retirement is peace of mind, knowing that your assets are well managed and protected.

Planning a good retirement is not only possible, it's practical. Where some people might want to sell you assets they're invested in to make a profit, I simply want to sell you on an idea. You can invest in diverse and low-risk assets that allow you to collect money when you need to and pay for your daily expenses, bills and any unexpected events. Then you can pass your money on in the most effective way possible when the time comes.

Some finance books promise to make you a millionaire. This book will teach you how to live on the retirement savings you have with the goal that you and your family can be comfortable for the rest of your days.

WHY TAKE MY ADVICE?

For starters, experience usually trumps any other asset. My name is Carl Feldman, and I've been specializing in retirement planning for over 30 years—since 1991. I'm the type of guy who gives every one of my customers my direct cell phone number—no secretary or landline to leave a message. This is important to me, because

INTRODUCTION

when any one of my clients has a crisis and needs support, I want to be there for them.

The retirement planning business is not and should not be about me, it's about you. My job is solely to offer the best possible advice for the people I serve. To be there for them when they need me. To help them plan and then protect their assets throughout their retirement.

All bragging aside, I have worked hard to ensure every plan I've created and amended has helped each family navigate retirement more successfully. I'm not here to make people rich by getting them to risk their money on growing a portfolio that has more risk than they can comfortably accept. I'm here to reduce risk, find as many assets that have protection features as possible, and then facilitate the most effective transfer of wealth as possible.

Outside of my experience, my advice is based on a number of credentials. It's my job (not yours) to stay up to date on the most recent advances, rule changes and laws that affect you and your assets. What I offer my clients is access to that knowledge any time they need it.

I also have official accreditations that have helped create my career: I graduated college with a Master in Business Administration in 1991, I'm securities licensed, and I created my own company—Feldman Financial Services, LLC—in 2000. In 2017, I started Feldman Financial Advisory Services as a registered independent advisor (RIA), and I am a fiduciary, which means I'm not beholden to any entities. Because of my fiduciary status, I'm also required by law to offer you honest and open advice with full disclosures, and to always put the best interests of my clients first.

I'm registered as a Life Underwriting Training Council Fellowship (LUTCF), and have my health insurance, property and casualty insurance, and Series 65 investment advisor licenses. In other words I'm positioned to help you with many of your specific retirement needs.

I would argue that, while credentials and licenses are important, especially a fiduciary who has your best interests in mind, it's also important to create a relationship with your financial services professional, so you can trust that person. Here's a bit about me personally.

I was raised in Brick, New Jersey, as the son of a Newark police officer of 31 years on the force. I played baseball, making the college team, where I became co-captain my senior year. I stayed on as assistant coach, then I earned my MBA from Wagner College, located in Staten Island, New York. I returned to my home of New Jersey, and I've been living in Lacey Township since 2007.

Work is important to me, and I prefer face-to-face meetings with people, so we can get to know each other. I'm always alert and available on my cell phone in case of a client emergency. But I do carve out plenty of time for my two daughters who are 13 and 15 years old.

I got into life insurance, because when I earned my postgraduate in 1991, there were many layoffs and a down market. Nobody was hiring an inexperienced kid fresh out of college. So I started my journey in financial services, working for Prudential Financial in Ocean County, New Jersey. Because that space is densely populated with senior citizens, I was dealing with many retirees. By my second year at the office, I was one of the leading agents.

You could say I found my calling in helping people on a daily basis. My goal is to put people in a better financial situation and help them stay there every day of my life.

What I learned at Prudential was that you could only sell Prudential products, not other products. This isn't a problem that's solely theirs; it's an industry standard for many large companies. Many employees were ignorant to this fact, but even if I knew there were better options to serve my clients, as a captive employee I was not allowed to sell those options to them.

INTRODUCTION

I would argue that big companies are often more concerned about what's good for the company than what's good for the people they serve. I started branching out and offering free seminars for people outside of work. I wanted retirees to get the facts. I wanted them to retire comfortably and have their money work for them, not for a big company.

In 2000, I branched out and started my own independent company, Feldman Financial Services, LLC. I wanted to become an all-inclusive service that would benefit many aspects of retirement. I want to show people how to make the most of their money by preventing their portfolios from going backwards at the hands of tax erosion. I can do this by reviewing tax strategies, creating regular income through annuity and life insurance plans, helping to plan for taxes that impact clients' estates and by helping to plan for my clients' overall legacy without paying out the nose for a lawyer's consultation fee.

I believe, the audience I serve best are people who are seeking reasonable rates of return on their investments. It is my experience that some people can get greedy at retirement and will keep trying to build their wealth, by taking, what I consider are excessive risks. In my experience this puts their portfolio and assets at risk for major losses. From my standpoint, many people who are looking to enjoy a secure retirement can be best served by my reduced risk approach. I tell every retiree that it's not how much you make but how much you get to keep. I specialize in tax strategies and reducing market losses to create a more stable retirement.

Being safe during retirement does not mean you won't make money. Many people miss out, because if you can help someone gain a solid 5 percent return every year, then they may be in a much better position than keeping their assets in a volatile market, especially if they cannot afford to take a big loss. Often my clients come out way ahead and have extra money, but when the market dips and other retirees lose a significant portion of their portfolios, my clients generally do not. That is because the customized plans I create are designed to reduce risk and avoid volatility associated with market swings.

Here's why that's important: If you start with $100,000 in assets and you make 30 percent in a year, then you're going to go up to $130,000. But if you lose 30 percent on that $130,000 the following year, then you're down to $91,000. It's amazing that you can lose more in the market than you can gain, even with the same percentages. Overall the market is a great place to grow your money over time before you retire, but after you retire, for many people it may not be a prudent place to have most of your assets invested, because the risk may be too high.

If you're the type of person who wants to have more money during your retirement and not less, then this book is for you. If you're the type of person who feels more comfortable knowing your assets are sheltered, rather than risking your retirement fortune, then this book is for you. If you would rather have up-to-date information with no conflicts of interest, then this book is for you.

From my family to yours, I'm grateful you've found this resource.

– *Carl Feldman*

1
WHY PLAY IT SAFE?

Retirement has changed significantly over the past few generations; yet many retirement planners offer cookie-cutter strategies, which have not changed. With fewer resources, pensions becoming scarcer, inflation raising prices on everything, a wild market with volatile up and down swings, and more strict rules and regulations, which may cause you to pay more taxes, you may have a challenge allocating your resources in the proper places to draw them out when needed.

Combine this with the fact that modern medicine is saving lives, and along with better food and enhanced safety features surrounding us, it's extending the average life span. It's a modern miracle that you could live longer, but this also means you need to stretch your resources for longer than most retirees did in the past.

Shifting policies can make retirement trickier to navigate, even if you're well read on what those policies are now. While a solid retirement plan is a sound decision, it's also important to build flexibility into your plan, like engineers do with skyscrapers, allowing them to wiggle during an earthquake or heavy wind. The good news is that many assets have shifted to meet the needs of modern retirement plans. Compare a slightly boxy Jaguar from the 1980s with wood trim inside and an oversized engine that got 12 miles per gallon to a sleek 2023 Jaguar with safety features, like airbags, lane departure warning, rearview cameras, and parking assist, plus an electric engine. They're similar but completely different.

It's entirely possible to find less risky assets, which reduce your exposure to market risk, meaning you may not lose half of your portfolio during a recession, even if your neighbors are. There are even some guaranteed income strategies* that you can leverage so that you protect your money from market losses, which is the name of the game during retirement.

As long as you can protect your assets and draw them from the right places when you need them and as long as you can pay the right amount of taxes by being in the right tax bracket, your plan will help your money last throughout your retirement.

It's amazing that people are willing to spend 30 or more years tucking money away for retirement, but often, these same people don't take the time to find out where that money should be. In

---

*Annuities are long-term insurance products primarily designed for retirement income. It is important to know a) that annuities and some of their features have costs associated with them like surrender charges for early withdrawals; b) that annuities used to fund IRAs do not afford any additional measure of tax deferral for the IRA owner; c) that income received from annuities and other assets may be taxable; and d) withdrawals from annuities prior to age 59 ½ may incur an additional 10% IRS tax penalty. It is important to remember that life insurance may require health underwriting and, in many instances, financial underwriting.

simply reading this book, you're taking one of the smartest first steps possible in retirement planning, which is learning about all the possibilities of minimizing risk to your nest egg and reducing the size and quantity of obstacles in your way.

I don't want to paint a grand picture and say that life will always be smooth sailing once you retire. It's always filled with its share of curveballs. But you can plan for those curveballs better by knowing what they could be.

Ultimately this book is designed to show you how to preserve your assets for the remainder of your years once you retire. You've worked hard for a long time, and retirement is when you get to continue enjoying the bounty of that labor until you complete your journey.

Armed with knowledge you should be greater prepared to create a safe and effective retirement plan that works as you need it to. My hope is that it should help you sleep better at night and enjoy more peace of mind, knowing your assets are exposed to less risk, and it should offer your family the satisfaction of knowing that you're doing well. It will offer you more control, so you can make more informed decisions about what to do in the event of any unfortunate circumstances. And a properly prepared retirement plan should last as long (or longer) than you do.

GAMBLING WITH YOUR FUTURE

On a warm summer evening, you can stand on the pier at Somers Point, New Jersey, and see all the way across the bay to the bright, shiny casinos in Atlantic City. These impressive man-made monuments are not monuments to winners at those casinos. They're monuments to losers. The casinos win because losers lose. The expression "the house always wins" is based on taking small wins here and there from everyone who enters the house, or casino. Even if some people win big, they slowly lose that money over time, like everyone else.

In the same vein, investing your money in assets that are out of whack with your risk tolerance may be seen as gambling with your retirement. While a nice moderate-risk mutual fund that tracks an index like the S&P 500 can be less risky and offer you a decent rate of return in the long run, it can still lose drastic sums. In 2008 to 2009 it lost almost 50 percent of its value; then it recuperated slowly to gain that value back in March 2013. In 2022 it dropped again by another 23 percent. These events are not outliers; recessions happen with some regularity. Surprisingly the United States experiences a recession about every 6 years on average, so it's likely to happen a number of times before and during your retirement.

My big question is this: Why are people chasing big returns and trying to get more money during their retirement? You've already done the hard work of saving up small sums here and there to get to retirement. At this point you need to protect the money you've made. Now you can cash in on your hard work if you play it safe. If you play the market too long, and stay invested in assets that are too risky for your tolerance you may eventually get burned by losing either small sums or having a big-time loss in the wrong market.

This doesn't mean you should take all your money out of investments and get any return on your assets. With inflation the most dangerous thing you can do is keep all your money in cash or a bank account. Inflation means that, every year, everything costs more. Sometimes much more, like 2022 when the U.S. Bureau of Labor Statistics told us the Consumer Price Index shot up to 6.5% for all items. If you hold on to your money as cash, it's going to be worth less every year. Yet cash can be the perfect asset to pay with if you have money in the market and the market is down. Otherwise, you could lose even more by withdrawing assets worth less than they should be.

The magic happens when you know how to allocate your resources, find the most prudent investments, and play it safe. This might not be the most exciting strategy, but it's the one that helps many people to ensure that their assets last the longest.

The best part is that with a good plan you will likely have assets that you can play with once the bills are paid. You can do whatever you want with these funds. You can put your extra money into the stock market—or take it to the casinos in Atlantic City.

WHAT'S AHEAD?

Many people don't want to think about their retirement until they're retired. The obvious problem is that it takes a specific plan and a little up-front work to make sure that you can retire comfortably for the entire duration. I understand that your interest level may be low and your time may be limited, which is why I've tried to make this book as much a direct "meat and potatoes" resource as you can possibly get. Everything in the following chapters is as short and sweet as it can be, with just enough information to make you aware of what you need to know to make the right plans and hopefully retire comfortably. But it also includes the maximum preparation and protection with the minimum amount of effort invested.

The following list includes the rest of the chapters in this book, with a brief summary of what you will learn in each chapter:

Chapter 2: Understanding what risk means for your future.
We will explore what risk means as far as your investments. Whether you're comfortable with more or less risk, in my opinion it's essential to not risk your money after you enter retirement. I

offer some guaranteed fixed income strategies* so that you gain some principal protection, even if the market goes down.

Chapter 3: Adding up your assets. It's important to know what you have, so you can properly allocate it in the right places and then take it out from the proper sources when you need it. Your assets are the foundation of any good retirement plan.

Chapter 4: Picking an income strategy. Switching from a steady paycheck—where you saved a portion of it—to living off savings can present a number of challenges for most retirees. As you switch from the accumulation of assets to the distribution of them, these best practices will help you navigate this new source of income.

Chapter 5: Understanding Social Security. One of the main sources of income in retirement comes from Social Security. But how and when you start collecting this resource is not straightforward, as it varies by person and plan. This chapter shows you how to maximize your benefits to get the most out of this valuable resource.

Chapter 6: Paying your fair share of taxes. Switching income sources can accidentally put you in a higher income bracket, which is one of the quickest way to lose more of your assets and your resources than you would like. Here we detail strategies to

---

Annuities are long-term insurance products primarily designed for retirement income. It is important to know a) that annuities and some of their features have costs associated with them like surrender charges for early withdrawals; b) that annuities used to fund IRAs do not afford any additional measure of tax deferral for the IRA owner; c) that income received from annuities and other assets may be taxable; and d) withdrawals from annuities prior to age 59 ½ may incur an additional 10% IRS tax penalty. It is important to remember that life insurance may require health underwriting and, in many instances, financial underwriting.

make sure you're paying your fair share of taxes, not someone else's.

Chapter 7: Insuring yourself against surprises. There are many types of insurance, some of which may be useful to you. Whether you choose to invest in different insurances, it's good to know what's available and how they can affect you, your partner and your family. The right insurance can protect your assets from erosion or total loss.

Chapter 8: Empowering women and individuals. Many aspects of retirement can be unpleasant to think about, although these are often the most important. This chapter details strategies for people who are on their own during retirement due to any number of factors.

Chapter 9: Protecting your legacy. Transferring your wealth at the end of your retirement is somewhere on the backburner to-do list for most people. The strategies portrayed here help you maximize the amount and efficiency of leaving your legacy for the people you love.

Chapter 10: Turning it into a plan. A solid plan has a foundation that incorporates all the above and includes enough wiggle room to pivot and stay safe during the unexpected. This chapter explores how to put together all the recommendations and advice in this book into a safe retirement portfolio.

Chapter 11: Finding a qualified financial services professional. There are a few good financial services professionals out there, and I want to ensure that you can find the right person for you. Steering clear of people with vested interests who simply want to take advantage of you and your money is possible once you know what to look for.

Chapter 12: What's Next? Your retirement plan should be as unique as your fingerprints, meaning it's designed only for you and your family's needs. This chapter explores the next steps you can take after reading this book so that you can create your own safe and lasting retirement portfolio.

THIS BOOK WAS WRITTEN FOR YOU

I don't know who you are, dear reader. But I do know that, like most people, you like to get assurances. There's no single retirement plan that works for everyone, which is why it's important to learn the nuances contained herein. What I do know about you is that you're human, and like all humans, you like to get your needs met.

The ultimate joy in life is not in getting, it's in giving. As we get older, we realize the importance of service and how it relates to our own legacy. For me that means offering high-quality information on the complex subject of retirement. I want to empower people like you to know more, so you can make better decisions for your life, which will ultimately affect the lives of everyone you know.

Please note that this book is filled with as much dense information as possible about a complicated topic; however, I've made as easy to understand as possible. Yet this is still just a book. I always recommend that you see an actual human (not some online robot) to get retirement planning advice. Any good financial services professional out there should offer you a complimentary initial consultation and aim to help you with the resources you have, not sell you on the resources his or her company offers. That professional should have your best interests in mind, not a larger company's.

If you're in the New Jersey area, I encourage you to set up a more in-depth strategy meeting with me, free of charge. If you have questions on this, you can always set up a free call with me. I wrote this book for you, and when you're done reading it, I will be here if you need me.

TRUSTING THE RIGHT PEOPLE

One of the pillars of your retirement portfolio is knowledge. Unfortunately the vast majority of people who "help" with retirement planning have a vested interest in the outcome and are not actually sharing knowledge with you—they're sharing products their company offers. Don't get me wrong, the industry should pay hard-working professionals to actually create a retirement plan and then update the client on any news or shifts in policy that might affect that plan. It's also important to have a relationship with a financial services professional so that, when you do have any questions, they're there to answer.

But many of these people offer their services with strings attached, meaning they're vested in selling you certain products that they and their company make money on. This means they are not acting in your best interests when advising you on which assets to get—they can't, because often their own company has a quota of products to sell you.

I've actually dedicated an entire chapter to deducing who is there to be of service to you and who is not. It's that important. Where you source your information from becomes important so that you have the assets you need when you need them.

Your allocation of assets should also change over time, so anyone selling you a product that may be good fit for you right now should advise you when to shift it into a different type of asset that's more useful for you in retirement.

A salesperson may not stick with you and let you know what you need for the long haul. A dedicated financial services professional should protect you and your assets, so that you always have enough throughout your retirement. One easy way of knowing if a person is dedicated to you or a company is whether he or she has certain credentials. A fiduciary is obligated by law to act in your best interests and to not sell you products without disclosing a vested interest first.

I'm a licensed fiduciary, and the information contained in this book is solely for your benefit. There are no offers, products, conflicts of interest or affiliate links or products of any kind. I do recommend that, once you've read the book and know more about your baseline strategy, you reach out to a financial services professional who does not have conflicts of interest. You are, of course, welcome to reach out to me to make a complimentary, no-pressure, no-sales appointment where we will discuss your assets and intentions. After helping you customize a plan that works for you, you can then decide if you would like to work with me or simply take the free information and plan that I offer, shake hands and part as friends.

You should be the star of your show, and your retirement portfolio should work for you and your loved ones. Anyone who's not supporting that agenda is likely selling you something. Please read through the rest of this book to discover more up-to-date strategies for creating a prudent and lasting retirement plan.

2
WHAT RISK MEANS FOR YOUR FUTURE

A husband and wife came into my office at the insistence of one of their friends—a satisfied client of mine. They had a more traditional situation, where the husband worked and the wife was a homemaker. He was retiring and his employer offered a retirement plan, which sounded great. However, he came in to see me just to check and see what my take was.

I pointed out that they had plenty of assets for the two of them to live a long, happy retirement, but their risk factor was surprisingly high. A downturn in the market could reduce their assets and limit how much money they had. Alternatively I pointed out a few safe assets they could diversify into that gave them a plan, which still made some money every year by leveraging fixed instruments. The upside may not have been as big, but the protection it offered, I felt, was phenomenal.

Between the rapport, my honest take on it, and their aversion to risk, they decided to get the guaranteed income plan. A few years later, Covid hit along with a huge recession, and the retirement plan the employer offered would have taken a 30-percent hit, which was a major chunk of their money. They called to thank me for switching them to the guaranteed plan, letting me know they had more than they need every month. Unfortunately their friends who were retired and still heavily invested in the market at higher risk lost a lot of money and would have to cut back on expenses.

This is one of many similar stories. I would say that most of these stories are deeply rooted in our culture and go back to the beginning of humankind. The Greeks told stories about people who were too proud to take advice, and so they suffered the consequences of their pride. Alarmingly some of us still need to learn our lessons the hard way today. Your retirement is no time to learn these lessons—it's your time to relax and cash in on your hard work.

John C. Maxwell famously said, "Fail early, fail often, but always fail forward." This is fantastic advice for young people. But in retirement, the game changes, and it's better to not fail. You spent your life learning lessons and pushing a figurative rock up a hill. Now is your time to finally count your victories and rest.

HOW TO SAFELY SWIM IN THE DEEP END OF THE FINANCIAL POOL

When you see a kid get into a pool, what's the first thing he or she wants to do? Swim to the deep end. It's where the action and excitement are. The hint of danger makes it all the more appealing.

As a metaphor the deep end of the pool is where we may find ourselves in over our head. If you're at the deep end of the pool for a half hour, it's great exercise. But if you're going to spend a few decades there, you might want to bring a life preserver or—better yet—a boat.

The scariest thing about finances and the future is risk. Ask any professional investor, and he or she will say that you must evaluate risk before making any financial decisions. Typically assets that have higher risk also have higher rewards, unless you lose. Assets with lower or no risk have lower rewards—but you can still lose due to inflation.

Here's an example: Holding onto the latest tech stock because it's consistently going up in value might seem like a great idea, since everyone else is making a lot of money on it. But if that company has a bad quarter, a bad year, or is part of a larger downturn in the market, you could end up losing quite a bit of money, especially if you end up needing that money to pay for something while the investment is down.

Holding onto a stack of cash might seem like a great investment, because there's zero chance that you will end up with less cash than you started with, but every year the US experiences inflation, which means the buying power of that cash decreases. While the average national price for a gallon of gasoline was only $1.11 in 1993, it's risen to $3.48 in 2023, only 30 years later.* Though there are rises and dips, everything gets more expensive over time, which means the value of the cash you are holding onto is worth less, because it covers less of your expenses.

The trick is not to be "all in" on the stock market or to only have cash. You can finesse your finances and get the most out of your money by making smart decisions on where you store your assets and when you take them out of storage as well as by diversifying what assets you're invested in. By reducing the

---

* https://www.energy.gov/eere/vehicles/fact-915-march-7-2016-average-historical-annual-gasoline-pump-price-1929-2015

amount of risk you're exposed to during retirement, you can more accurately assume that your money will last longer, will be less exposed to market risk, and will lose less in the long run as you withdraw some of your assets as income.

But perhaps the most powerful outcome of reducing your risk is increasing your confidence.

PEACE OF MIND

Ninety percent of the people I sit down with say they're conservative or moderate investors. They don't want to take on a lot of risk. But when I look at the assets they're holding onto, they actually have huge risk throughout. The reason they're holding onto so many risky assets is because someone smart about money that they trust gave them investing advice, which may have been great preretirement, but it may be way too risky during retirement. They're often invested in blue chips that have historically showed tremendous gains but, on the flip side, have also shown steep losses during certain periods.

When you reach retirement, your mode of income changes from earning an income and saving for retirement to drawing on those retirement savings as income. That in itself is pretty wonderful. But beyond that you can also shift your mentality.

If you've always been worried about having enough for retirement, then you must set up a retirement plan that clearly shows how much you currently have in assets and get an accurate estimate of how much you will have as a monthly income throughout your retirement.

This type of planning is more than just crunching dollars and cents and letting you set a monthly budget for yourself. It may actually decrease the amount of worry you have about finances, which can increase your peace of mind. For instance, a person who doesn't know how much he or she has, where and when to draw assets down, or how long his or her money will last will probably worry about finances throughout retirement—in other words the rest of his or her life. I don't know about you, but that doesn't sound appealing to me.

On the other hand, if you did know all those details and it was part of a plan that had guarantees* and safety mechanisms built into it, then you could let go of all that worry and instead spend your time enjoying retirement. To me that's the main goal of creating a customized, solid retirement plan. Yes, the numbers are important. But that irreplaceable feeling of contentment for the rest of your life is priceless.

Go to any public swimming pool, and you will see that the happiest kids are the ones swimming in the entire pool, deep end included. The reason they can swim in the deep end is because they know that they can swim well enough to navigate it and enjoy it. Most of those kids had a swimming instructor of some sort—whether it was their parents or a swim coach—to help them develop those skills and feel confident in the pool.

WHAT'S YOUR APPETITE FOR RISK?

Most people are taking on more risk than they realize, especially in retirement. To help you understand why certain assets are risky and why others are considered safer, I always have people who want to meet with me fill out a "Color of Money Risk Analysis" form. This helps you reveal your own attitude about money and

---

*Annuities are long-term insurance products primarily designed for retirement income. It is important to know a) that annuities and some of their features have costs associated with them like surrender charges for early withdrawals; b) that annuities used to fund IRAs do not afford any additional measure of tax deferral for the IRA owner; c) that income received from annuities and other assets may be taxable; and d) withdrawals from annuities prior to age 59 ½ may incur an additional 10% IRS tax penalty. It is important to remember that life insurance may require health underwriting and, in many instances, financial underwriting.

your assets changing in value, especially if they're prone to lose value.

It's common to hear that people are more upset about losing money than they are happy about gaining that same amount of money. It's called *loss aversion**, and it's a cognitive bias, which means it's hardwired into people's brains. Basically you are likely to be twice as upset when you lose money than you are happy when you gain money.

Beyond that you have limited resources after retirement. If you take a loss on your portfolio and need to take money out when the market is down, it's much more expensive and hits you much harder. Earning 20 percent on a $100 asset one year will bring it up to $120. But losing 20 percent on that same investment the next year will lose you $24, bringing you down to only $96. Or imagine losing 20 percent on $100 and ending up with $80, then gaining 20 percent on that same asset the next year and ending up with $96. Risk leads to bigger losses than you think, unless you've diversified your assets and have set up some asset protection in your retirement plan.

This doesn't even take into account drawing down your assets and taking money out of the market when it's down, which pokes larger holes in your pocketbook.

You can see how mathematically and psychologically the cards are stacked against people who are hoping to grow their portfolio during retirement in the same way they were doing this beforehand. I like to find what's in every person's best interests for investing during retirement. This usually means setting a certain percentage of your portfolio into fixed income strategies, which are guaranteed, then tucking away a portion of your assets into whatever you want to take a risk on, since then you will at least have a large enough safety net to withstand a market downturn.

---

* *https://thedecisionlab.com/biases/loss-aversion*

FINDING THE RIGHT RISK LEVEL FOR YOU

Once you know your personal limitations around risk, then you can start tallying which assets you have and transferring them into storage or other asset classes so that you can draw them down when you need them.

It's important to determine your risk tolerance so that you can figure out how much you're able to take on, how much you need to take on, and how much you are willing to take on. Risk tolerance is like building a house. First you put down a solid foundation, not the roof. Without a space to build on, nothing will work. If your retirement plan is expecting 20 percent return on your investments, then what happens when you don't get that? Or what if you get 6 percent one year and then lose 20 percent the next?

The year 2022 was a historically bad year, with an overall 20 percent market loss.* For anyone deeply invested in the market, that's a large chunk of your life savings. Market fluctuations are beyond the control of the average investor. You can't control the market. In my experience many retirees don't actually need the extra assets added to their portfolio during retirement, so I'm a big advocate for reducing risk as much as possible. Playing it safe might not seem like the most appealing strategy for you, but when your neighbor's portfolio is down 20 percent and yours is doing just fine and actually gaining year after year, you will see the value in guaranteed investments and reduced risk.

Partly your retirement isn't the same as your parents' or grandparents' retirement. Only 30 years ago, many people had pensions, which offered guaranteed payments for the rest of one's life. With the drastically reduced number of pensions, you now have more choices and take on more risk with a 401(k), but a lot of it is unnecessary risk. We may have another 2008 recession

---

* *https://www.cnbc.com/2022/12/29/stock-market-futures-open-to-close-news.htm*

happen, and people could lose 30 percent or more of their money. Would that be a big enough loss to bring you out of retirement and force you back to work?

A retired woman came into my office for a meeting one day. She had retired with $600,000 in her 401(k). She let her husband manage the finances, and he left all the money in the market, so it could grow. Unfortunately only one year into retirement her account was down to $495,000 due to a drastic market fluctuation. During the past few years before she retired, everything had gone up in value, but now everything was suddenly going down. Because they did not have diverse investments, they were forced to draw down from this account and take out more money than they expected. Every dollar in the account was only worth 82 percent of what it had been a year earlier, which meant every dollar they spent cost them almost 20 percent more!

If you want to swim in the deep end of the financial pool, you should absolutely do what makes you happy. However, you should also have the ability to swim back to the shallow end when you need to so that you can take a break. Once you understand the risk involved in staying invested in volatile spaces, you may want to set a large chunk of your assets in a safer harbor, which typically offers lower returns but significantly reduced risk. Then you can swim back to the deep end any time and play there as a part of your overall experience, without needing to stay there for the entire time where you could sink.

3
ADDING UP YOUR ASSETS

Your assets are all the valuable resources that you've spent a long time putting toward your retirement. Where these assets are allocated and when to spend them are some of the trickiest parts of setting up and then living out a safe retirement plan. But once you understand the concept and put everything in motion, you will find that it's not unbearably complicated.

As you enter retirement, you will discover that the right strategy is just as important as the actual dollar amount you have saved. That's because retirement is not as simple as saving dollars in a shoebox and then spending those dollars. If that were the case, you would probably run out of money sooner than you think, fewer people would be able to retire, and there would be a lot more shoebox theft.

Fortunately we have created financial systems to help take care of retirees, if you know what to look for, and where to look.

TYPES OF ASSETS

When most people think of retirement assets, they usually jump to their 401(k) plan. Perhaps, ironically, some people think this is a poor retirement asset, but it's a great way to save money for retirement. Here are the different types of assets you may have in your retirement portfolio:

Social Security. This is a guaranteed monthly amount that you will receive, based on how much money you (or your spouse or parent) has paid into the fund. People who have lower savings and higher needs may collect Supplemental Security Income.

Annuities. These may come from your employer or may be a product you choose to invest in. These offer you guaranteed monthly or yearly income. However, there are many types, with plenty of rules, regulations and possible fees. Be mindful of what type of annuity you invest in, knowing the pros and cons and whether it fits your portfolio. A fixed annuity is guaranteed to earn at a certain rate, while a variable annuity follows market changes.

Pension plan. This is a defined benefit plan your employer may offer to reward your loyalty in working for and staying with their business for a certain amount of time. While these have decreased significantly, they're still being offered to many federal employees and some companies.

Traditional IRA. These are not taxed when you deposit funds into them, but they are taxed when you pull money out of them. You're banking on taxes being lower in the future than they are now. You will be subject to a required minimum distribution (RMD), which will require you to take a certain amount of money out of this account after age 73 or face hefty tax fines.

Roth IRA. These are taxed when you deposit funds into them, but they're not taxable when you draw money out. Additionally you don't need to add this income toward your taxes during retirement, and you can forego RMDs.

Retirement Savings (including 401(k), 403(b), and 457 plans). These are similar to IRA accounts, except that 401(k) plans offer a higher contribution limit, while IRAs typically offer more investment options. For instance in 2023, the contribution limit for a 401(k) is $22,500, or $30,000 if you're older than 50, while the contribution limit for an IRA is only $6,500, or $7,500 if you're older than 50.

Other savings. You might also have money invested in savings accounts, checking accounts, brokerage accounts, cash deposits (CDs) from the bank, or bonds. You may even have cash sitting in a shoebox under your bed. No judgment, but you want to make sure the bulk of your retirement savings is safe.

DIFFERENT ASSET CLASSES

Once you add up your assets, it's important to look at the risk for each one. You might not think that holding onto cash has risk, but consider this: As inflation rises the value of your dollars decreases. It's good to have some cash set aside for when you need it, but it's also important to be earning some level of interest on your assets so that you can match or even outpace inflation. While the stock market increases about 10 percent per year, or 6 to 7 percent if you account for inflation, it can vary wildly from year to year. That means some years it may be up 30 percent and some years it could be down 30 percent. What that means for your money is that if you need to take out cash from your investments on an up year, your money is worth 30 percent more—but a disaster during a down year could cost you an extra 30 percent.

The way I see it, your assets are either safe, or they're not. Here are some examples:

SAFE

Cash or bank accounts. This money will lose value to inflation, but overall you will always have one dollar for every dollar bill you hold onto, whether it's a physical bill or in your bank account.

Cash deposits (CD). This money is even more safe than cash, because these can often earn enough interest to counter inflation.

Bonds. Government bonds are guaranteed and offer a fixed interest rate. Private bonds can be risky, depending on the company, but overall these tend to be a safe bet.

Social Security benefits. This is monthly income for all retirees and is considered guaranteed income for as long as the plan is in place. It will make up a portion of your monthly "income" during retirement, so that you're not constantly drawing down your savings.

Annuities. These pay out a monthly or yearly income for retirees until your death, so that you know you can count on another fixed amount added to your portfolio.

Pension plans. Similar to Social Security benefits, this is an additional monthly payment you receive until you pass away. You can count on a fixed dollar amount, which makes this a safe bet.

ASSETS WITH HIGHER RISK PROFILES

Traditional and Roth IRAs. The market is volatile and can easily rise and fall double digits in a single year, especially lately. The USA experiences a recession on average every six years, so you should expect a few during your retirement. These are great vehicles for saving money for retirement, but during retirement you should rethink how much you want invested in the market because it's simply not safe.

401(k)s. As mentioned earlier you may have tens of thousands, hundreds of thousands, or even millions of dollars in your 401(k) plan. Volatility means that if you need to draw money out, you never know how much that asset will be worth at the time.

Cryptocurrency. Even more volatile than stocks, this type of money is largely untested. They offer the promise of huge reward but also offer high risk, with some cryptocurrency falling up to 90 percent in a few months' time.

This doesn't mean you should only have low risk assets in your retirement portfolio. Some of the assets that have greater risk can also bring big rewards. However, you can have an overall conservative portfolio if you can allocate your necessary monthly income using low risk assets and then sink some of your extra assets into the high risk category to wait out the market and collect when the time is right. These high risk assets are a way to get much more money than you initially invested. Yet it's important to have an exit strategy with assets that are high risk unless you plan on leaving these as a legacy gift.

Additionally if you have a spouse and you are both retiring, it's absolutely essential that you pay close attention to partner benefits for Social Security and pension plans. You often only get one chance to make a decision about this, and it could affect the rest of the spouse's retirement, should the beneficiary pass away first.

TURNING ASSETS INTO A PLAN

Once you know how much money you have and where it's located, you can start to formulate your retirement plan. When you sit with a financial advisor, he or she can listen to what your retirement goals are and let you know how that will work with the assets you have. For instance if you intend to travel and spend a lot during retirement, that's perfectly fine, as long as your plan can support that. If not you will either need to add more money into your retirement portfolio or rethink how much you plan to spend monthly. Otherwise, you run the risk of running out of money during retirement.

Your plan should account for risk. No matter what your risk tolerance is, focusing on guaranteed income is great, because it provides you a level of security. The name of the game during retirement is to never go backward, because you simply may not have the time it takes to recoup market losses. A solid retirement plan should have diverse assets that you can draw on when you need them and that will not take a big hit if the market changes.

4
INCOME STRATEGY

Prior to retirement you likely earned a paycheck and balanced your monthly budget based on how much you and your spouse earned. A portion of that income went toward saving for retirement. What I see in most retirees is that, although they may not need the same monthly amount they were earning (because they no longer need to make that retirement savings payment), they still enjoy getting a similar paycheck.

During retirement you will earn an "income" based on your guaranteed monthly payments, such as Social Security benefits, pension, annuities, and the like. You make up for any deficit in what you need by drawing down your saved up resources, which can be your cash, bank accounts, IRAs or any other assets you are holding onto. It's also good to have a fund that covers any unexpected expenses.

Strangely this is actually a difficult thing for savers to do. They've spent their lives getting to retirement by saving whenever possible and putting money into various assets. It can be hard to flip the switch and take that money out instead.

How much monthly income you allot for yourself depends on your needs and goals for retirement. And those change over time. When you are no longer working a day job and have time to travel, you may want to see the world and spend more early on. As your children have children, you may want to spend more time with your grandchildren. As your body ages and you get into your late 80s and 90s, you may want to spend more time at home, because it's not as exciting to spend 12 hours sitting on an airplane.

When in doubt, overshoot: Plan for the maximum income you would like to spend, because switching from a steady paycheck, where you saved a portion of it, to living off savings can present a number of challenges for most retirees. As you switch from the accumulation of assets to the distribution of them, these best practices will help you navigate this new source of income.

ACCUMULATION PHASE
This is the phase before retirement when you were storing up your assets. Hopefully you had a nice chunk of money in assets, like the market, that grew over time. Because we usually have 40 or so years before we retire, the market can be a great place to use the power of compound interest to expand how much you have.

DISTRIBUTION PHASE
When you retire you will no longer save money for retirement. Instead you will be drawing down some of your assets to provide monthly income for yourself. These are added to your fixed monthly income so that you always have the amount of money you need.

SEQUENCE OF RETURNS

This is where things can get complicated for your assets. If you have much of your assets tied up in the market prior to retirement, the market can govern how much money you have at the moment you retire. This is why it's a good idea to speak with a financial advisor and get your assets looked at prior to retirement. Then come up with a retirement plan that includes shifting assets from one space to another.

For instance you have a nice little party with your colleagues, and they wish you a happy retirement. You're 65 years old, and you have $2,000,000 in your IRA account. It seems like a solid amount of money for you and your spouse for the next—hopefully—30 years. But within a month of your retirement, the market takes a hit. That year the market loses 30 percent, and your IRA drops to $1,400,000. You just lost $600,000 of your money in a single year. The next year the market dips a modest 15 percent, and you now have $1,190,000 or 59 percent of your original retirement savings. You don't get to keep adding money to this account. You just have to pray that the market turns around, and you can get that money back. Meanwhile you're spending almost double, because for every dollar you pull out of this fund, it's only worth 59 percent of what you expected it to be.

This is called a bad sequence of returns, and anyone who retired just before a recession or depression experienced it. It's surprisingly common. However, it's also possible to mitigate the damage by shifting your assets from the market into lower risk alternatives. It's also possible to get a good sequence of returns and end up with more money than you expected. But I always shoot for the minimum amount of money you need, and anything extra is a bonus.

When it comes to investments, my question for almost everyone who sets up a meeting with me is, "Why chase a big return on your investment if you don't need it?" Here's what I mean by that: You can probably set up a comfortable amount of monthly income for yourself without taking a big risk, like staying heavily invested in the stock market. Sure the stock market can perform really well and has historically performed well over time. But in your retirement, do you need to grow your account by 30 percent, 40 percent or even double what you have? Or would you have all your needs taken care of by keeping the amount you've already collected?

I ask this because if your money is tied up in volatile assets, you can see the opposite happen and lose 30 percent, 40 percent or even half. The market has big dips. It happens. Even to smart people with good intentions. Because of the possibility of losing so much money, is it a risk you will feel good about taking and will not be nervous about throughout your retirement?

To put this into perspective, if you gain 30 percent on your $100,000 investment, you will have $130,000 the next year. But then if lose 30 percent that next year, you're down to $91,000. Losses are a bigger hit than growth, and they're more devastating during retirement. The most important thing for your retirement portfolio is to never go backward.

The most devastating thing is being unprepared for market volatility and needing to take out money—or being forced to take out money due to RMDs, when the market is down. It takes too long for that money to go back up, if it ever does. A 30 percent loss on $100,000 gives you $70,000. It takes a 42 percent return to build back to $100,000. If you're still taking money out of that account, you might not be able to build it back up. It's a vicious cycle.

We've been experiencing a fairly nice rise in the market since 2008; however, when the market crashed that year, people experienced a 38.49 percent loss on the market. Anyone who was heavily or entirely invested in the market lost nearly 40% of their portfolio in a single year. Some of these people had to continue working until 2016 for their market assets to come back to where they were. Can you imagine the thrill of retiring, but then going back to that same job or trying to find a new job, if your position was already filled, and working another eight years? Doesn't sound like the start of a great retirement to me.

The worst possible scenario—and this actually happens all the time—is that panicked investors sell off their stocks when the market crashes to the bottom. They switch everything to cash, fearing the worst. Unfortunately they then miss the rebuilding phase, where all those investments begin going back up in value. They take that massive financial hit, then sit on cash, and don't get back into the market until the stock prices have risen again. The general philosophy in stock market trading is to buy low and sell high. But these people sell at the low and then buy high. But hey, someone has to be the person helping Wall Street fat traders get rich! Do you want that to be you?

One person I've had the pleasure of helping with his portfolio retired from a major pharmaceutical company. He had much of his money in his own company's stock in 2006, which is noble, but I warned him about the lack of diversity in his portfolio. When he recognized this, he diversified 75 percent of those assets into some lower risk assets outside the stock market and kept only 25 percent in his company's stock. Two years later the market crashed, and that 25 percent of his portfolio took a big hit. But he came to me and said, "Carl, if we hadn't done what we did, my portfolio would have tanked. I have more money than I did 14 years ago when I started seriously saving for retirement, and I was able to continue my retirement without any problems. A lot of my friends retired and ended up with only a fraction of what they started with before 2008."

Trust me it's not about tooting my own horn and being right. It's about you being safe during retirement and protected from any possible financial hardships.

NEED MONEY VERSUS WANT MONEY

During any recession or depression, people are faced with some brisk realities. What are the essentials that you need? And what are you spending on things you want? It's important to distinguish these two, because it's possible to reduce your wants, but it's less possible to reduce your needs.

For instance food is a need. You must eat to live. But do you need to go to fancy restaurants? That's more of a want. You need a place to live, so your house is a need. But new landscaping for the front yard and backyard is probably a want. Getting your backed up plumbing fixed is definitely a need, but renovating the bathroom with tile is a want.

Your portfolio should fully take care of your needs. From there you can focus on your wants. So when we start to make a retirement plan for you, we can say that you have different options for staying invested in assets that are earning, while also staying flexible enough to cover any unexpected expenses that arise. Beyond simply low risk and high risk assets, let's dig into how people can grow these assets over time:

Allocate how much low risk money you have. Hold onto this for when you need it, such as a home repair or purchasing a new car. If your high risk assets are up in value, use those instead and enjoy the windfall.

Add up your guaranteed monthly income. This is your Social Security, pension, annuities and other guaranteed sources of income you may have.

Set aside some money in moderate risk assets that are relatively stable and can grow a little over time.

Once you're set up with an appropriate amount of monthly income that you can use when you need it, then allocate some of your assets into long-term assets that have more fluctuation and can be riskier but also offer higher rewards over time.

What is that magic number of monthly income that will make you happy during retirement? That's where it's important to plan out what your need money is. Cover your expenses first. But this is also your retirement, so think about your want money, too—that's for your enjoyment.

There are a number of assets I recommend to clients that offer safe, monthly income. These help you budget better. Imagine only using a portion of your wealth to guarantee income for the rest of your life. The repurposed dollars you make during retirement can go to more want money spending, play the stock market and growing your money further, or passing it on to your children and grandchildren. There are many options for what you can do with your money, but once you have a guaranteed income, the money machine keeps producing money, and your needs (and often your wants) are financially covered.

One of my clients came to me with a sizeable portfolio, shopping around to find the best financial advisor. I recommended a guaranteed income stream if the market went up or down, which would mean the product offered certain protections for market volatility. That was promising for him, but it was especially promising, because he could still do whatever he wanted with the majority of his portfolio. As it turned out, the other firm he talked to didn't offer him options or ask what he was interested in. They simply recommended that he purchase a number of assets. He ended up investing with me, and now he has more money than he started with and keeps saving. He also has his monthly expenses taken care of with the payouts his plan had set up for him.

SPOUSAL CONTINUATION

Many retirement portfolios are designed for two. Yet often there's only one person designing the plan. I prefer to keep everyone in on the conversation, even from the planning phase. Traditionally, although not always, it's the husband who does the finances. This has led to many situations I've witnessed (outside of the circle of people I work with) where the woman is left to fend for herself or suddenly has to take a massive pay cut if her husband was the primary breadwinner and didn't consider what would happen if he passed away earlier—even though women tend to outlive men.

Spousal continuation is often an option for assets, like social security, annuities and pensions. It generally means you take smaller payments now when it's both of you, but if the beneficiary passes away, then the spouse continues to receive even smaller payments, which is still more than receiving nothing.

While it is important to consider your overall health when thinking about spousal continuation, accidents happen and illnesses can suddenly come from seemingly nowhere. I've known couples where the woman was in poor health all her life but lived well into her eighties, while the man was sturdy as an ox, then suddenly passed in only a few weeks' time after discovering a major illness. You can plan for the possibility of death, but you can never truly prepare for the emotional shock of it happening. When this trauma combines with major financial losses, it can be devastating.

A solid retirement plan must address both spouses in all scenarios. Then they will remain financially stable, even if they're emotionally upset.

ASSET MAXIMIZATION

The barebones basic formula you're looking to create in a retirement plan is to make sure your living expenses are covered. I

LIFETIME INCOME PLAN

$	LIVING EXPENSES	
	INCOME	INCOME GAP

eliminate the income gap

also recommend adding a little buffer for the various just-in-case scenarios that are likely to happen. To make sure you can enjoy your retirement and live in comfort without constantly worrying about money, you simply need to eliminate any income gap between what your living expenses are and what your "income" is, which are your monthly payments, plus assets you are drawing down from.

One simple way to do this is to reduce your living expenses. By retirement many people own their home and have reduced or paid off their mortgage. Perhaps it means setting a comfortable and enjoyable budget and sticking to it, relatively speaking (vacations aside or budgeting for vacations as well).

THE TRANSFER PHASE

As all good things come to an end, eventually both you and your spouse will pass. A safe retirement plan also considers who your legacy will benefit and how they will receive it. This keeps in mind how much your beneficiary will be taxed and what types of assets they will receive. If you're a baseball fan and have collected numerous rare cards worth a lot of money, they might be more valuable to you than they are to someone who is not interested in baseball. If you have collected a number of complex assets, it's a good idea to have a plan in place where those can be transferred to the beneficiary and their value can be made known.

Many times I have actually witnessed clients grow their savings throughout their retirement beyond what they started with! If you have enough monthly income to cover your needs and continue to grow your wealth—even modestly—throughout your retirement, then you, too, can pass on a fortune to the people you love most. Growing your wealth and passing it on seamlessly is generally made possible and even simple by trusting in a qualified retirement advisor who can help you budget and set up wealth-transfer vehicles for the people you designate.

Understandably all these may seem like a lot. This is not like taking your car in for an oil change. It's more like designing and building a car, then maintaining it over the next 30 years. Enlisting an expert designer to help you build your retirement portfolio and then maintain it for the duration of your retirement takes that burden off of you. This professional can help not just with the legal logistics, which can be read in a book, but with the experience of having done this exact thing hundreds, or even thousands, of times. Would you feel safe driving a new car you built yourself if it was the first time you had ever built a car?

5
UNDERSTANDING SOCIAL SECURITY

For most retirees Social Security will be your main monthly source of revenue that you can rely on. It's essentially a fund that people pay into throughout the duration of their career. You have probably noticed a Social Security tax bracket when you file your taxes. You are funding your retirement as you pay this tax.

When you retire it's your turn to collect this monthly paycheck. As long as you've worked for 10 years in the United States and have not missed filing your taxes for three consecutive years, you are a likely a candidate for collecting Social Security and letting the current work force pay their taxes into this fund, so you can enjoy your retirement. If you have not worked for 10 years or you were a stay-at-home parent for instance, you may still qualify, depending on your spouse's eligibility.

Despite the fact that most people collect Social Security and rely on it to replace their paycheck, there is a deep lack of understanding about this benefit. How and when you start collecting this resource is not straightforward, as it varies by person and plan. Fortunately you can find out how to maximize how much you get, so that you can make the most of it.

WHEN TO COLLECT SOCIAL SECURITY
Your Social Security benefit base pay is calculated by taking how much money you earned while you were part of the work force and paying into it. The average indexed monthly earnings (AIME) calculates your last 35 years of earnings to create an average index of your monthly earnings. Fortunately you can take your higher earning years and use those to predominantly determine this. Because most people's salaries change over time, this usually means taking the most recent number of years into account, so it can be good to collect a higher wage for longer.

Once you've calculated your base, then that number is reduced or enhanced by when you choose to begin collecting Social Security paychecks. You can start collecting as early as 62 years old, which means you would collect for the maximum amount of time but for the minimum amount of money. You can also defer your Social Security payments until you're 70 years old, which would mean you would collect for the minimum amount of time but for the maximum amount of money. That duration and payment amount changes every year, depending on when you decide to collect or defer.

Here's an example of how that looks for a person whose base pay is $1,545 per month at full retirement age, which in their case is 67 years old (the calculation depends on your birthday). The "Age" column is when they collect, the "Monthly Benefit" column is how much they collect, and the "Lifetime Benefit" column assumes they continue collecting until they pass away at an average age of 87 years old.

AGE	MONTHLY BENEFIT	LIFETIME BENEFIT*
62	$994	$326,841
63	$1,078	$335,870
64	$1,186	$349,772
65	$1,296	$361,321
66	$1,410	$370,444
67	$1545	$381,696
68	$1,684	$389,948
69	$1,828	$395,128
70	$1,975	$397,192

If they decided to collect Social Security early at age 62, they will get $994 per month or $326,841 over the projected lifetime of the benefit. If they collect at the full retirement age of 67, they will get $1,545 per month or $381,696 over the projected lifetime of the benefit. If they delay collecting until age 70, they will get $1,975 per month or $397,192 per month. The longer you defer your benefit, the higher it is. Delaying your benefit may increase the amount by up to 8 percent per year. This can be a good option for married couples with uneven income, where one person is gaining more spousal support for life through Social Security benefits.

However, this doesn't mean that deferring your Social Security benefit is right for everyone. If you're ready to retire early and want to make up for your income gap in between your monthly expenses and cash flow with this money, then this may be the best option for you.

What's the best option? You can actually get a Social Security Maximization Report that addresses your situation and shows options that work for you, so you can figure out when to collect.

This will help you maximize this asset. At Feldman Financial Services, LLC, we offer this report free of charge when you book a meeting with us to discuss your retirement plan. This is a major foundation of many people's retirement, so it is a big deal to get as much as possible. You deal with Social Security first, then the other assets afterward.

TAX-PREFERRED INCOME

Your income still gets taxed—yes, even in retirement. Taxes are one of the biggest expenses retirees face that slowly erode their assets. A major benefit to your Social Security income is that it's considered "tax preferred," which means you only pay taxes on 85 percent of it. That means 15 percent of it is untaxed. Within one year if you earn under $25,000 as an individual or $32,000 as a couple filing together, you do not need to pay taxes on your Social Security benefit.

This may not seem like a big boost, but as you will find out, your goal in retirement will be to keep your tax bracket lower so that you can pay only your fair share of taxes and not someone else's.

COST-OF-LIVING INCREASE

A question I frequently hear from people nearing retirement is that they're worried their Social Security benefit won't cover their costs because of inflation. It's a valid concern, as US inflation tends to increase the costs of goods and services a little over 3 percent per year. Fortunately the good people at the Social Security Administration have already thought of this and raise the payment amount based on inflation.

For instance in 2022 there was a 9.6 percent cost-of-living increase. For some people who experienced a major increase in health care costs, that hit home, but for others the particular goods and services they use didn't rise much. Regardless the Social

Security benefit was raised to make sure retirees have enough money to pay their bills. That means that every Social Security beneficiary, regardless of how much they bring in, experienced a nice bump in their income.

That being said Social Security alone is not designed to replace your full income, unless you plan on living under the poverty level. It's just a piece of the retirement puzzle. Granted it's a solid first step to figure out how much you could be bringing in and when to collect it, so you can then start fitting the other pieces together.

6
PAYING YOUR FAIR SHARE OF TAXES

You spent your life paying taxes, which is why you get nice retirement benefits like Social Security. Unfortunately you still spend the rest of your life paying taxes, even in retirement. Thankfully there are clever assets that allow you to stop paying taxes on income you've already paid taxes on.

Contrary to the belief that you need to pinch pennies during your retirement, a common predicament retirees end up in is paying too much on their taxes, because their retirement income was so high. This happens when you don't plan your taxes ahead or you don't have the proper accounts to draw money out of.

Sometimes it happens because when you hit the 73-year-old milestone, you have to take RMDs from a traditional IRA or 401(k), even if you don't need the money. The tax penalties are sometimes up to a hefty 50 percent if you choose not to take this money you're supposed to take. This can lead people to collecting money at inopportune times, then needing to use that money to pay the extra amount they owe on taxes, since their income level increased and they owe a higher percentage.

Your goal in retirement is to pay your fair share of taxes and not someone else's. Uncle Sam wants to make sure the country is funded, along with all the great programs that you will likely benefit from. But that tax money should be collected fairly and distributed across the great many people in the work force, too. At this stage in your life, you want to protect your assets from eroding, and taxes are one of the biggest factors in diminishing a retirement portfolio.

TAX BRACKET

If you've ever filed your own taxes, you've likely seen that, because you make a certain amount of money, you now owe a certain percentage in taxes. The more you make, the higher that percentage. There are different methods that people use during their careers to keep their tax bracket lower, such as donating to charitable causes and finding various write-offs.

During retirement you're subject to the exact same brackets. But if you've set up a solid retirement portfolio with diverse assets to draw from, you have more options to make sure you can keep your bracket as low as possible.

For the year 2022, paying taxes in 2023, the following seven federal income-tax brackets will apply to you, at varying stages of your income: 10 percent, 12 percent, 22 percent, 24 percent, 32 percent, 35 percent and 37 percent. Let's explore how much money you must make (or draw down to create retirement "income") to qualify for each bracket.

PAYING YOUR FAIR SHARE OF TAXES

2023 tax table: single filers

Tax rate	Taxable income bracket	Tax owed
10%	$0 to $11,000.	10% of taxable income.
12%	$11,001 to $44,725.	$1,100 plus 12% of the amount over $11,000.
22%	$44,726 to $95,375.	$5,147 plus 22% of the amount over $44,725.
24%	$95,376 to $182,100.	$16,290 plus 24% of the amount over $95,375.
32%	$182,101 to $231,250.	$37,104 plus 32% of the amount over $182,100.
35%	$231,251 to $578,125.	$52,832 plus 35% of the amount over $231,250.
37%	$578,126 or more.	$174,238.25 plus 37% of the amount over $578,125.

2023 tax table: married, filing jointly

Tax rate	Taxable income bracket	Taxes owed
10%	$0 to $22,000.	10% of taxable income.
12%	$22,001 to $89,450.	$2,200 plus 12% of the amount over $22,000.
22%	$89,451 to $190,750.	$10,294 plus 22% of the amount over $89,450.
24%	$190,751 to $364,200.	$32,580 plus 24% of the amount over $190,750.
32%	$364,201 to $462,500.	$74,208 plus 32% of the amount over $364,200.
35%	$462,501 to $693,750.	$105,664 plus 35% of the amount over $462,500.
37%	$693,751 or more.	$186,601.50 + 37% of the amount over $693,750.

2023 tax table: married, filing separately

Tax rate	Taxable income bracket	Taxes owed
10%	$0 to $11,000.	10% of taxable income.
12%	$11,001 to $44,725.	$1,100 plus 12% of the amount over $11,000.
22%	$44,726 to $95,375.	$5,147 plus 22% of the amount over $44,725.
24%	$95,376 to $182,100.	$16,290 plus 24% of the amount over $95,375.
32%	$182,101 to $231,250.	$37,104 plus 32% of the amount over $182,100.
35%	$231,251 to $346,875.	$52,832 plus 35% of the amount over $231,250.
37%	$346,876 or more.	$93,300.75 plus 37% of the amount over $346,875.

2023 tax table: head of household

Tax rate	Taxable income bracket	Tax owed
10%	$0 to $15,700.	10% of taxable income.
12%	$15,701 to $59,850.	$1,570 plus 12% of the amount over $15,700.
22%	$59,851 to $95,350.	$6,868 plus 22% of the amount over $59,850.
24%	$95,351 to $182,100.	$14,678 plus 24% of the amount over $95,350.
32%	$182,101 to $231,250.	$35,498 plus 32% of the amount over $182,100.
35%	$231,251 to $578,100.	$51,226 plus 35% of the amount over $231,250.
37%	$578,101 or more.	$172,623.50 plus 37% of the amount over $578,100.

As you can see, there are two larger jumps between these increments: From 12 to 22 percent is a drastic increase, and from 24 to 32 percent is another. You will likely fall neatly between those two. If, for some reason, you have a major expense and must pull out extra savings, which then turns into "income," you could accidentally set yourself up for a major unexpected tax payment in addition.

To prepare yourself for this possibility, it's time to find out how you can keep your tax bracket low, while getting the income you desire.

WHAT DOESN'T GET TAXED

Holding onto some emergency cash or a CD in the bank is a highly liquid asset. You can access it any time and use it to pay major expenses (check on your CD to make sure early withdrawal penalties don't apply). You don't get taxed on cash that's actual cash or is in your checking or savings account. You don't get taxed on cash that's in a CD, although you will be taxed on any interest earned.

This is important, because if you're suddenly faced with a major home repair and need to take out $40,000 in assets to cover a new roof, you get to choose where that money comes from. If it comes from your cash account, this will not be treated as income, so you will not have your tax bracket suddenly raised by $40,000 in extra income that year (even though you spent that money on a new roof and paid taxes on the job).

ROTH CONVERSIONS

Roth IRAs and other Roth assets get their taxes paid off before they accrue interest. This means you won't have to pay taxes on that income when you cash in on your asset, which is great in and of itself. On top of that, you don't need to claim the income on your taxes. So no matter how much you take out, it will not affect your tax bracket.

Roth assets are one of the best ways to keep your tax bracket as low as possible. Throughout the year you can plan for how much money you will need and your base levels of income. Then simply take out some of your Roth income to fill in any gaps as needed, and you can still maintain a nice, low retirement income level.

You can even pass on your Roth assets to beneficiaries during your estate planning when you leave your legacy to your loved ones. Then they can enjoy an income tax-free asset that's converted to their name.

If you didn't start saving your assets in a Roth account, don't panic. You can undergo a Roth conversion to turn some of your assets into Roth assets by paying taxes on them. There are a few rules and restrictions involved, such as not being able to collect on these assets until the account is at least five years old and you're past the age of 59 and a half years old. This is best done with a professional retirement advisor to help you with the nuances involved. If you choose this route, I always recommend you have the cash on hand to pay the taxes and do not draw from the account itself to pay them, especially if you end up paying a penalty.

In 2023 taxes are lower now than what we expect in the future, so converting to a Roth could be a good choice for you. In 2025 they're reverting back to a higher tax bracket as some of the tax cuts from the Tax Cuts and Jobs Act of 2017 expire. We feel there is a good chance that taxes will increase in the future, so if you do a Roth conversion while taxes are lower, you can reap big benefits. Currently you can take assets, like stocks, bonds and mutual funds, and convert them while the market is lower. There's no limit on Roth conversions. However, there's a $6,000 to $7,000 limit (depending on your age) toward your Roth IRA in cash. This makes sense for most people and is especially smart for younger people, because they have depressed assets. This is another reason to work with a financial professional. We can look at your unique situation and help you determine if it makes sense to pay taxes now for tax-free money down the road.

TRADITIONAL ASSETS

If the market is doing great and you want to take out some of this money to cover expenses, it may be as good a time as any to cash in on these. You can take out a little extra to make sure you have the bandwidth to cover the extra taxes, too.

Alternatively when the market is down, it may be a good time to do a Roth conversion. When you convert your assets, you only pay taxes on the current value of the asset. If your $10,000 shares are suddenly down to $6,000 and you pay taxes on that $6,000, when the asset goes back up to $10,000, you still only paid taxes at the lower rate, and the increase in value of the asset is now yours tax free.

WRAPPING AROUND YEARS

At the end of any year, if you have "wiggle room" in your tax bracket, you can draw down out of any taxable asset that's doing well and switch to cash, or a non-taxable asset. This continual rebalancing will help you prepare for the year ahead, so you can continue to keep yourself in a favorable tax bracket and reduce your tax payments in the future.

If you are facing a major cost, such as a new roof, you can also ask if you can make payments over time. If you're able to take out some money during the year you made the purchase and some money on January 1 of the following year, you can claim that "income" on the following year's taxes. A $40,000 roof split into two years then only raises your income by $20,000 for each year.

PLANNING YOUR ASSET DISTRIBUTION

On paper this sounds easy. In real life your accounts and expenditures are constantly fluctuating. Knowing which accounts to take money out of, rebalance money into and stay in the proper tax bracket could be exhausting. Or you could partner with a financial professional who can help you plan your taxes in advance and pull out the right assets from the right places when you are facing a major expense.

Understanding where you stand is essential. If you're trying to make your retirement portfolio last you for the long haul, then this is a critical component.

That being said many people I speak with have done their taxes and are aware of the generalities of them. But they're not well versed in taxes during retirement. And why would they be if they're not retired yet?

Most people think they've already earned their money and paid their taxes. They want to take big chunks of money out of IRAs and 401(k)s without understanding how that choice will impact their taxes and bump them into a bigger income tax bracket, which could cost them tens of thousands of dollars more in a single year.

If you didn't plan for one-third of your retirement portfolio to go toward taxes, then you may take a big and unexpected hit, which could alter the quality and enjoyment of your life. This shocks many people, when I tell them that.

STAYING UP TO DATE

I recommend finding a retirement advisor who will keep you in the loop about any upcoming changes that will affect your assets and who will be there to answer any questions you have around these changes. For example the biggest recent reform is the Patient Protection and Affordable Care Act. As far as IRAs go, everything is the same. Your RMD starts at 73 years old and not

70 ½ anymore. Everything else is business as usual. But we need to see what the new tax laws will be in 2025. They shift over time and can affect your assets and overall portfolio.

Taxes have gone up and down over the years. Historically any time the government needs money, they raise taxes. There are many government programs that they're responsible for financing. It's not political that they gave out money during the COVID-19 recession to benefit people who lost income and businesses. But now we have to deal with the fallout of what happens when that influx of money hits our economy. This likely means more taxes in the future to make up for the deficit.

We will have to deal with new tax laws, and there will be some changes. People who adapt to what exists now have the opportunity for gains by reducing their future tax obligations by putting money into Roth IRAs and Roth 401(K)s or converting some of their IRAs into Roth IRAs now while taxes are relatively low.

7
INSURING YOURSELF AGAINST SURPRISES

Because car insurance is required for anyone who drives a car, everyone walks into my office with some experience regarding insurance. As an overall concept, insurance is a way of making sure that you're safe and covered no matter what happens. If you're driving a car and you have insurance, you're safeguarded against mistakes—whether a driver hits your car or you hit another car. Beyond that insurance has options that cover all kinds of things, such as protecting your windshield from getting cracked by a random stone that pops up from someone's tire. You won't be able to charge that person for it, because they won't even realize they've launched a stone at your windshield—in fact you will likely not even see where it came from. If you didn't get the optional full coverage, you could pay $2,000 out of pocket if they have to recalibrate any sensors, but if you did opt for full coverage, it's a small copay.

The concept of insurance is simple: You pay a given monthly amount to protect against something. If that thing happens, you're covered by insurance, and there's a small copay. The deeper value behind it is that you can get peace of mind. If something unexpected happens, you won't be financially ruined. With cars it's fairly simple. You're guarding against hitting a much more valuable car and being on the hook to pay tens of thousands or hundreds of thousands of dollars for it. You're covered if an uninsured driver ends up hitting you.

But insurance goes well beyond cars and for a good reason. There are much more expensive things that have actually incurred devastating losses for people who were not expecting such big out-of-pocket expenses. Knowing what things you may want to insure to protect your portfolio empowers you to make the best decisions for your own portfolio, so that you and your partner are financially protected and everyone can enjoy peace of mind, knowing that you have a plan in place.

HEALTH INSURANCE

One of the most frequent concerns I hear from people who are about to retire is how they will be able to continue to get good health care and maintain health insurance during retirement. It's a very valid point, because health tends to decline rather than improve with advanced age. Whatever health challenges you may have been facing are likely to be exacerbated by discovering new ailments. This is more something to be aware of than something to be nervous about. If you know you're already experiencing many expensive health care issues, then it's a good idea to make sure your insurance reflects that. However, just because you have not faced any serious health complications yet does not mean that you should not have health insurance.

There are affordable health care options out there, for anyone who does not have an employer with an insurance program that covers you during retirement. The key to choosing the right health insurance plan is making sure that your basic needs are covered first, such as by reducing any co-pays and including any medication you know you will be using frequently. From there you also want to make sure that you can reduce your out-of-pocket expenses so that health care doesn't erode your retirement savings.

Medicare is similar to Social Security, since it is a federal program that you have paid into throughout your career. Just like Social Security, you want to maximize this benefit in retirement.

Medicare is split into four parts:

- **Part A: Hospital insurance.** Covers the costs of health care at medical facilities. Offers coverage for medically necessary inpatient care at hospitals, skilled nursing facilities, hospices and some home health services.

- **Part B: Medical insurance.** Covers the costs of health care outside medical facilities. Offers coverage for doctors' services, hospital outpatient care, mental health and some preventative health care services.

- **Part C: Medicare Advantage (MA) plans.** Policies you can purchase from certain private insurance carriers that provide the same (or more) coverage as Parts A and B.

- **Part D: Drug coverage.** Prescription drug coverage offered through private Medicare-approved insurance companies.

Many people with Part A do not pay a premium, because they have already paid enough into the system. As with Social Security, a certain portion from each your paychecks is deducted to pay for

Medicare. When you've had Medicare tax withheld from you or your spouse's pay for at least 40 calendar quarters, then you may be eligible for free Part A coverage.

The monthly premium associated with Part B is set according to income level, although most people will pay a standard monthly premium amount and a small yearly deductible. Individuals who have an annual income greater than $85,000 and couples who have a joint annual income greater than $170,000 will have an extra charge added to their premium due to their high income level. Parts C and D are provided via private insurance companies, so the monthly premiums of these policies depend on the extent of their coverage and can vary between companies.

Outside of Medicare many retirees choose to stay with their private insurance for a number of reasons. Perhaps they want to stick with a doctor they know and like or have the certainty that their plan already works for them. As long as this is within your budget and you allocate money for it, sticking with the insurance you're already on can be a good plan.

LIFE INSURANCE

Many people don't understand the core concept behind life insurance. It's not just leaving enough behind to cover the cost of your own funeral—it's actually a tax-efficient wealth-transfer vehicle that you can leave behind for either your spouse or the beneficiaries you choose.

When people are younger, it's more important to get life insurance for income replacement on a spouse. Who passes away early. Especially if the spouse was the breadwinner, it's essential to have enough money to replace income and figure out a plan from there.

As you get into retirement, life insurance has a lot of other uses than replacing income, since you're no longer earning a paycheck. By paying in a monthly premium, you can create and maximize an estate plan that's tax free for your beneficiaries. Unfortunately I would estimate that 90 percent of people don't understand how life insurance can benefit them. They see it as an expense and not as an opportunity. Even if you pay a monthly premium, it's not always an expense. The cost benefits and tax benefits of life insurance properly used in a portfolio is undervalued and thus underleveraged. If people would be more open to learning more about it, they would see many benefits, such as their money growing tax deferred, with payouts that could be tax free.

The problem may be because the life-insurance industry itself has changed over time, and what people tend to think about first is a model that didn't work well for others in the past. We now live in a new generation of tech-savvy people. Only 30 to 40 years ago, we had stationary home phones and pay phones, but now we have mobile phones that can make calls, text, take photos, check email and much more. There's little comparison between the two. Similarly life-insurance policies of the past did not have the same growth potential savings feature that new policies have. Most people don't know about all the products out there, and they're worried about unnecessarily spending money on something they can't benefit from. Once people sit and look at the new plans and see the opportunities for wealth transfer that are open to them, they see the benefit to their loved ones.

One of the things I got specialty training in was to write life-insurance policies for my clients. The key is having an open mind. I help people solve problems. I don't just look at a product that will make money and then sell it to the people I work with. I discuss the options with each individual to see what we need and how we can accomplish those goals by finding or creating the right products for them. It's like using a toolbox, we work with various tools to shape each retirement plan. Life insurance is one of those key tools.

LONG-TERM CARE INSURANCE

One of the hardest-hitting expenses during retirement is long-term care. That doesn't mean that you must have insurance for it, but if you don't have an alternative plan, it could easily wipe out your assets. The problem is that few people think they will need long-term care, because they are in good health now. The reality is that over 70 percent of retirees end up needing long-term care and needing it for an average of over three years! This long-term care costs an average of $60,000 per year for professional in-home health aide services or over $100,000 per year for a private room in a nursing facility. Places with a higher cost of living could be significantly more.

Choosing to get long-term care insurance means that you and your spouse will be covered in the event that either or both of you need care, without financially wiping out yourself and your partner. Remember that if you or your partner require long-term care and you have savings tucked away to cover it, this may be considered "income," depending on which asset you're drawing from. This means it could also boost you into a tax bracket you don't want to be in.

There are packages where you can get life insurance with accelerated benefits that can protect you from long-term care expenses. The best scenario is to speak with a specialist who knows how health insurance, life insurance and long-term care insurance fit into any safe retirement portfolio. These professionals can help you make the best decisions for how insurance products can support your lifestyle.

8
EMPOWERING WOMEN AND INDIVIDUALS

Without rocking the boat too much, there are some biological differences between men and women. The fact that women get pregnant and give birth and men do not means that women end up needing to take more time away from their career than men do. That leads to a slightly shorter career on average, which also means less time to save money for retirement.

Whatever political standpoint you have, we have also typically experienced a culture where men are paid more, which has led to the man often being the breadwinner in a relationship, even if the woman is also employed. Please note that these are generalizations, based on long-standing traditions. Women have often become stay-at-home parents and have spent years of their career life caring for their children. Additionally many times the finances and budgeting are left for the man to take care of.

This is changing, but it has been the pervasive norm for so long that it's the reality for a significant majority of the retirees I meet with. It's in no way a judgment or statement about our culture; it's simply an observation of facts. The reason I bring it up is because it can heavily affect how women thrive throughout retirement, especially if they have not been in the know about their financial situation or plan until their husband passes away.

There are many easy fixes to any retirement plan that cover either partner when one spouse passes first, but these fixes must be implemented at the beginning of retirement. These fixes can range from when and how to claim benefits to setting up funds, to allocating assets or to making sure both parties are covered. Even though statistically women live longer than men, it's still a possibility that either spouse could pass first, so it's good to set up safeguards just in case.

EMPOWERING WOMEN

Many women retire alone, whether by choice, due to a deceased spouse, or due to any other number of reasons. It's just as important for a woman to speak with a professional retirement planner as it is for a man, because money doesn't discriminate. However, consider this: The pay gap by gender in 2021 was that women only earn 82 cents for every dollar that men earn.* This means that, over a career, there's simply less overall money to save, which can lead to smaller portfolios to manage. This also means it's even more important for women to ensure they're making the most of that money during retirement.

---

* https://www.gao.gov/products/gao-23-106041#:~:text=For percent20example%2C%20in%202021%3A,18%20cents%20on%20the%20 dollar).

Your knowledge is your power. Reading this book is part of that knowledge base. But on top of that, it's important to find a professional advisor you trust and stick with him or her, so you can learn more about things that apply specifically to your situation.

If you are retiring as a couple, it's important for both the man and the woman to be involved in the planning process. It's essential that they both know the working details, where assets are stored, and what benefits a spouse will receive if and when the other passes first.

If you find yourself in a situation where this was not how your portfolio and plan was set up, it's just as essential to seek out a qualified professional. He or she can help you figure out which assets you have and how to allocate them for your best benefit. You can always create a new retirement plan, especially when a spouse passes and your needs change.

THE RETIREMENT ADVISOR RELATIONSHIP

In the United States, 72.3 percent of retirement advisors are male*, which is actually an improvement in equality over the past. This may be why women are less likely to trust male retirement advisors and are more likely to seek female retirement advisors for council. The same applies when roles are switched: Many male retirement advisors with an old-school mentality tend to stay away from single women, because they assume women can't make decisions and will make difficult clients.

As times change and both men and women become more empowered and educated about their finances, these stereotypes are slowly eroding. I work with many single women who are widowed. For me it's just as essential to explain everything in a way that they can understand as it would be when I am taking on a male client. Whether the client is a man or woman, you have to care for your

---

* *https://www.zippia.com/finance-advisor-jobs/demographics/*

client's needs first. When I do retirement planning for couples, I always make sure both parties are present so that they both know what the plan is when one inevitably outlives the other.

No matter what your feelings are around the differences between men and women, it's important to note that a solid retirement portfolio should cover both people in a relationship and should not be biased to your sex. It's customized based on your spending needs, family situation, lifestyle, assets and much more—none of which has any preference over men or women.

Often by the time I end up speaking with a widow who comes to me for retirement-planning advice deep into retirement, that widowed spouse was unfortunately never part of those essential financial conversations when she should have been included. This doesn't mean it's too late to take control of the financial situation, but it is a shame that more people don't learn about their retirement plan or possible scenarios where they will be in charge earlier on.

For example there's a widowed woman I work with. She has no pension and low Social Security, but she's maintaining a $1 million-plus retirement portfolio and has been for the past 20 years. What we decided was that a safe portfolio that offered guaranteed returns would be the best option for her, and as it turns out, the plan has been working well. So far her portfolio is still maintaining and the money she originally held onto is safe and secure, despite the radical market volatility we've experienced. For the future I advised that she could comfortably take $50,000 per year and the money would still last from ages 80 to 100. This plan worked out great for her, knowing she's covered for the rest of her life and will still have assets to pass on to her beneficiaries. Managing assets and expectations is the primary goal. Though she feels bad for her other retired friends who lost lots of money in the market, she's content with her own decisions and solid retirement plan.

9
PROTECTING YOUR LEGACY

How will people remember you when you are gone? Perhaps your life's work has changed the world, and you will be sainted. But for most of us, our children and grandchildren remember us, because we left behind a legacy of loving and caring for them—plus a bunch of money when we pass. Thinking about your own mortality is usually the last thing anyone wants to do, but the messes that happen when someone does not have a clear legacy in place can shift how people remember you. If you don't have a plan, then you can expect for otherwise great people to fight over the details of your death, such as how you should be taken care of and who your assets should go to.

Fortunately there are strategies for you to easily take care of this well in advance. It's called your legacy planning, and it's the final step to making sure your retirement portfolio is complete. Once you and your spouse have enjoyed your assets throughout retirement, the goal is to pass your assets to your beneficiaries as tax-efficiently as possible so that you and your beneficiaries get the most out of them.

True story: A very sweet older woman walked into my office. She didn't have much, but she had allocated $40,000 that she wanted to split between her two sons. As it stood the money was in two CDs at her local bank. The sons would both be taxed on this money, so each would earn a fraction of $20,000—likely in the $14,000 ballpark. Now this sweet lady was in good health, but I discussed the benefits of a good life-insurance policy to transfer that wealth rather than using cash. As fate would have it, she did pass away only three years later (in her late 70s), but instead of leaving each son $14,000, she was able to leave each of them $56,000 in tax-free money. Obviously that's more than the original $40,000 she began with. When it comes to passing on your assets, it's about knowing the most efficient method and designating it properly.

TAKING CARE OF YOUR SPOUSE

One of the hardest parts of my job is delivering death claim checks to widows and widowers. Death is a sad but essential counterpart to life. There are no guarantees that can keep you or your spouse safe and alive. But there are guarantees in the form of insurance that your assets can transfer smoothly from one spouse to the other and that the surviving spouse will be taken care of financially, despite your absence.

Think of it this way: When a loved one dies, we are in shock. It's unthinkable that this could happen, and it can be emotionally devastating. The last thing we need is compounded stress with knowing what payments to make or where income will come from. It's essential for both spouses to be in on a clear plan to be financially protected in case of death.

I've seen the impact of making sure assets are there to pass on. Money is no replacement for a lost spouse, but it always helps people to financially navigate a difficult time.

Part of this conversation involves making sure you set up any Social Security benefits, annuities or pensions to cover a spouse in case of death. This may mean that you collect slightly less while both spouses are alive, but it also means you will not financially cripple the other when you pass. Unfortunately most of these choices are irreversible, which means you choose one option for life.

It's also important to make sure both parties know which assets exist and where they can be accessed, that each has a recent will in place to allocate where their assets go to, and that both parties are covered, even if one has chronic health conditions and the other does not.

A LEGACY OF SELF-SUFFICIENCY

Part of your legacy is your ability to take care of yourself financially. Something I take pride in is that I've never had any of my clients run out of money and end up with nothing at the end of their lives. I've helped people modify their plan over the years and have set people up in government programs. I've helped structure where money is allocated and drawn from, and I've always tried to included ways in a client's plan for them to have something to pass to the next generation.

Having a legacy is not just because it feels good to pass on something to loved ones, it's also so you and your beneficiaries have peace of mind that you managed your money well and could preserve your retirement.

A financial advisor can help you make the best decisions that work for your retirement lifestyle. Albert Einstein (a pretty smart guy) said that compounding interest is one of the greatest inventions in history. Letting interest compound on itself over time is very powerful. When you combine that power with certain tax-deferred vehicles and abilities, you wind up having more money and hopefully a smaller tax burden. Which is designed so that you can pass it on in the end. With compounding interest, you get growth on top of growth, and later on when you take a distribution, you can pay down the tax and still net more money.

It's not unusual that I've seen many people pass away with more money in their accounts than they came to me with—and it wasn't because we put everything in the market and got lucky. Luck has almost nothing to do with long-term financial gain, if you're doing it the right way. Instead we often use the power of IRAs or annuity products that get tax-deferred growth or tax advantages. An annuity can be tax deferred and taxable on withdrawal, but the growth over time can be greater than if you got taxed on the fund since you started.

Now time is the biggest factor involved in compound interest. If you started saving $500 per month for retirement when you were 18 years old and put it in the market with a 10 percent annual growth rate, you would end up with over $7 million at full retirement. Compare this to the fact that if you saved up $500 in cash every month for that same duration and there was no compound interest: You would only end up with $300,000, which is less than 4 percent of the compound interest amount.

For everyone who's not 18 years old, you can still grow your money steadily over time. Whether your retirement portfolio needs to last you for three or 30 years, the plan should include the maximum duration. Playing it smart and safe means that if you overshoot, you end up with more assets to pass on to the people you love.

Honestly the majority of wealthy retirees I work with never brought in big incomes. They squirreled a little away every year, and now in their 80s, they have a lot of money, because they were smart about leveraging interest and then shifting their strategy during retirement. They also kept more of their money by using clever tax strategies and drawing from the right assets.

WHAT CHANGES TO MAKE

With just a little tweaking to your portfolio, you could leave a substantial legacy to the next generation. Especially if you leave it in the right way and keep your mind open to possible wealth-transfer vehicles. Over time they've changed the IRA beneficiary rules. Imagine, rather than receiving a lump sum that hasn't appreciated yet, you could send your grandchildren a check every year, even 30 years after you're gone. This is possible.

Some people work hard to show their children they can have a better life. That's a great way to be a role model. But it's also nice to pass on a chunk of change to them. They can then save that money and grow it for their retirement. You might discover that there are numerous tax-leveraged products and there are fantastic wealth-transfer vehicles that can be utilized now.

Life-insurance policies can be a means of efficient, guaranteed returns*; can protect your assets from erosion by providing long-term care benefits; and can also become an incredibly efficient wealth-transfer vehicle. In that sense life insurance can be an estate and finance protector against the most common financial hits to your assets, which affect a large swathe of our population as we age.

---

* *Annuities are long-term insurance products primarily designed for retirement income. It is important to know a) that annuities and some of their features have costs associated with them like surrender charges for early withdrawals; b) that annuities used to fund IRAs do not afford any additional measure of tax deferral for the IRA owner; c) that income received from annuities and other assets may be taxable; and d) withdrawals from annuities prior to age 59 ½ may incur an additional 10% IRS tax penalty. It is important to remember that life insurance may require health underwriting and, in many instances, financial underwriting.*

One critical reason that most people make mistakes regarding their legacy is that they were never given the right information, so they weren't able to make the best decisions for themselves. Most people are turned off by life insurance, because at some point, a salesperson was hounding them to sign a policy that was probably too expensive and may not have been a good fit for their situation. The perception is that there's no way a life-insurance policy can benefit you while you're alive, but there are some great products out there with a lot of living benefits. You just need to find them with a qualified advisor so that you can make informed decisions.

Nobody likes paying for car insurance, unless you have a car accident. Healthy people don't want health insurance until they need to pay large expenses and see how much was paid by their insurance. Imagine how much money you spend on any given weekend of entertainment. When it comes to protecting your estate, wouldn't you rather keep yourself and your loved ones safe by spending a few extra dollars? How you spend your money is a decision every individual needs to make for themselves. All types of insurance have expenses, but what it comes down to is ensuring that your life or the lives of the ones you love are maintained or improved if something unfortunate were to happen. It could become the smartest decision you ever made.

THE LEGAL THINGS NOBODY LIKES TO THINK ABOUT

Probate is the process of settling an estate after you pass away. It can be confusing and complicated, depending on your estate, the amount of your assets, and how they're titled. It can also be simple. No matter how they are set up, everyone's beneficiaries still have to go through the process.

Certain products like IRAs, annuities or life-insurance contracts can help people avoid probate, because they have designated beneficiaries. They go directly to these people. Some clients

I've worked with had up to two years of tax complications on their estate, which created a massive headache for an executor to process. Most of the time, a few complications can't be completely avoided. If you can be proactive and go through everything you own in advance, review your estate and assets and then put a named beneficiary on everything.

That's an excellent time to see a professional advisor. I tell people all the time that you can see an attorney and have a discussion about this, and they will charge you $350 an hour. Or you can have this discussion with me free of charge, and I will point you in the right direction, which may also be with that same attorney but perhaps not. Attorneys get paid handsomely by the hour to go through probate. An unscrupulous attorney may even put assets into the estate unnecessarily, when these could be settled outside the estate easily.

Don't get me wrong, attorneys have their place. But you need to understand that, with estate planning, it's better to keep it simple and efficient. Otherwise, a large sum from that estate could go to the attorney. It doesn't take much time or money to set your ducks in a row before you die. Your grieving family will be grateful to have everything in writing so that it's easier for them to process your death and to not deal with a legal headache in the middle of losing you. It also could help eliminate any fighting between family members or beneficiaries after you're gone.

10
TURNING IT INTO A PLAN

Knowing what to do and doing the thing that needs to be done are two different things. If you were supposed to plant seeds in the garden in late spring, because it is the best time to do so, but you waited until late summer, you're going to end up with a completely different harvest. The seeds won't have time to grow up and produce the fruits, vegetables and flowers you want them to. Similarly your retirement plan should be a cornucopia of wealth for you, your spouse and all the beneficiaries you designate. But it can't do that unless you're willing to take a little action now to make it happen.

No matter what advice you get, you're the one who has to make decisions. You plant the seeds. Your plan should have enough wiggle room that you and your spouse can enjoy a nice, long retirement together, no matter what happens. That's the key: Planning for the unexpected, since something unexpected will inevitably happen. If you have a plan, then that means you're prepared. But if you're unprepared, it means you did not have a solid retirement plan.

MAKING SURE YOU DON'T OUTLIVE YOUR ASSETS

People come to me nervous that they will run out of money during retirement. I deeply understand that concern, because partly the issue is so big that it's hard to fathom and the consequences are so severe that it could mean ending retirement by going back to work or not enjoying retirement, because you have to strictly budget and live on less.

Having a conversation about financial services is like learning a foreign language. The industry that profits off retirees pumps out misinformation dozens of times a day. There are also well-intentioned people who love you but don't know anything about retirement planning and are offering anecdotal advice. They may say something like, "Leave all your money in the market, I know someone who stuck with Tesla and made a hundred times return!" Well that's exciting but possibly inaccurate and, otherwise, a very lucky break that's not repeatable by everyone.

Your finances, assets and you and your spouse are all unique, and every household has different spending levels. You need advice on a case-by-case scenario that's customized to you. You don't need one-size-fits-all generic advice that may not suit your needs.

Imagine your brother had a stomachache and went to the doctor only to discover that it was a ruptured appendix. Does that mean that the next time you have a stomachache, you also have a ruptured appendix? It's very unlikely.

TIMING IS EVERYTHING

I speak with people of any age, at any time. When most people seek an advisor to help them with retirement planning, they're tied up with kids or grandkids: They are watching their kids graduate from high school or college, or they are seeing their kids get married and have their own kids. There's never an ideal time to sit down and talk about retirement planning. You have to make that time for yourself. It's only a few hours, and you will thank yourself that you took the time to do it.

Truthfully you should not wait until you're retired to think about retirement. The sooner you take care of some things, the better. Imagine discovering you had cancer, and you were able to take care of it safely and naturally while it was still small, before it took hold. Alternatively if you wait until stage four and it's spread throughout your body, your options are much more limited.

As long as you've been saving some money for retirement, you're going to be better off than if you have not been saving any. But you still need to know how much you have overall, so you understand how much you're able to draw every month and stay financially secure through an uncertain future.

I work with an incredibly kind couple who are both retired. They have a special-needs child who is 35 years old and unable to care for himself. They take a longer-term view of his care and their financial assets to know that he will be okay, even after they're gone. As they grew closer to retirement, they built his care into their plan, because it's one of the things that was most important for their specific needs.

The sooner you secure riskier assets into assets with less risk, the less likely you will experience a financial catastrophe during your retirement. Waiting to shift all your market money until after you're retired could be a massive hit if the market is down when you retire.

FINDING THE RIGHT BALANCE

People are creatures of habit. We tend to focus on the urgent thing, like taking out the trash, because it's trash day. You can't ignore taking out the trash, or else you're going to have a toxic mess on your hands. But you also can't ignore your retirement until it smacks you in the face.

We put everything into a plan so you always know what to do, no matter what happens. You don't have to worry as much about a down market where you might sell off your assets in a panic. You don't have to worry as much about an up market in hopes that you can sell at the peak. You don't have to worry as much about any of that. You just have to make a prudent plan and stick with it. Stop thinking about your money, and enjoy your retirement.

The reason we do that is because it's hard to comprehend anything longer than a few days or a week. Even a year into the future at times seems unfathomable. Imagine 30 or 40 years from now. This could be you at the end of your retirement. People are living longer these days, and if that ends up describing you, that's great news! Enjoy your extra-long life. You just want to be sure that your money serves you throughout that duration, especially if you need more medicine in the future.

Not long ago when I was in school, I drank from a drinking fountain, like every other kid at that school. Only a few decades later, my kids and all of their peers bring fancy water bottles to school, with the highest-quality water. The future brings big changes, which are especially hard to adapt to the older you get. Older people now ask grandchildren to help them with overly complicated phones that have too many buttons and features. Even if you're savvy now, it may take you by surprise one day in your 80s or 90s that things have shifted beyond your ability or desire to keep up with them.

Having a trusted advisor educate and explain anything to you in a way that makes sense is important so that you can continue making good decisions, even when things change. For instance most applicants want to communicate with people via email, but I work with people who often don't have email accounts. They got an education and worked for 50 years without an email account, and most of their friends are on email. Yet companies still try to force them to use email. Even using a computer is a task for some, if they grew up using a typewriter.

It's normal to want more money for your retirement, and it's possible. But placing your fortune in the stock market could incur significant losses, which you may not be able to make up again. I've noticed that people tend to take bad advice when it seems like they can profit from it. Marketers know that and use it as a lure so that they can dupe you into buying risky assets that are not likely to perform well. I guarantee that if I doubled your assets now, you might be happy you had more money, but it wouldn't change your lifestyle that much. If I halved your fortune now, you would definitely feel the pain. Every big bet and promising payout comes with a flip side, so be prepared to take a big loss if you're still chasing big gains.

GETTING IT RIGHT THE FIRST TIME
Fortunately as a retirement advisor, I can confidently tell you that I can help you with all the complicated computer stuff. Even with 30 years of experience in the field, I use some of the latest software to help you determine when is a good time to claim Social Security benefits, how to manage your assets and pensions, how much risk you have compared to what you would like to have, and how long your money will likely last you at varying levels of comfort. When you hire an expert to help you with a job, you get it done with greater craftsmanship in less time.

Sitting down with a financial advisor is like accessing the best parts of almost a decade of education and training and then applying them toward your situation.

The biggest takeaway is that no matter what you choose to do, you do not want to go backward in retirement. It's much harder to earn that money back when you need to take distributions, and it usually leaves you with significantly less than you want.

WHEN TO SEE A RETIREMENT ADVISOR

When most people sit down and work on their finances with me, they're skeptical at first. It takes a lot to win someone's trust. I'm a facts guy. I like to present options and possibilities. I don't ever present something that's not a good fit for your portfolio; I'm legally bound to only offer you products that are in your best interest. But there's something very human about connecting over money—people get emotional about it.

This is your life savings. This is your nest egg. This money needs to last you and your spouse for longer than you live and then hopefully help set up your kids' fortune. Much of what I do could be considered as much counseling as it is advising. People want to be heard. You probably want someone to actually listen to you.

That's what a good advisor does. They listen. They learn what you need. Then they offer their genuine advice on how you can do it best. Sometimes you just need a calming person in your life to show you options and offer you comfort and peace of mind. That's why I give my cell phone number out. People sometimes call me in a panic about things they don't understand, but then in a matter of minutes, I can help the anxiety go away, because I can listen to them, connect with them, and show them a good strategy, if that's what they need.

There are a lot of pushes in the financial world to automate things and use robots. But honestly a robo-advisor may not be able to translate things for you, unless it's into a different language. The financial services industry speaks in what can seem like a foreign language. We have jargon and specialized language that doesn't mean much to the layperson. We have regulations and requirements that are important to think about long in advance and not give you a beeping alert 10 minutes before you need to make a critical decision. I speak plain English to people and break down what they need and don't need, based on their specific portfolios and plans.

Creating a trusted relationship with an advisor is part of your retirement plan. It means you will have someone who understands you; who takes time getting to know you as more than data, as a real human; or who can offer solace when a tragedy happens, and we need to shift your plan together.

This is so much more than just being able to see your accounts online. While that function can be useful, it can also be distracting or even worrying to check them every day. So much technology these days is trying to prove how smart it is, validating its own existence. My philosophy is that if it's helpful, great. If not move on.

Computers can handle complex math equations, but beyond that, they fail to grasp human existence. A computer can tell you the sum total of your assets, but it can't do the most humane thing and actually care if you're going through a tough time. The human element is irreplaceable—at least for now. Even if you have a computer do your taxes for you, it doesn't mean they're catching things that an expert tax consultant can easily find.

GO WITH THE FLOW

Now this might seem contradictory, since I always recommend being prudent and planning, but it's also good to maintain a bit of flow in your plans. A woman I work with just turned 90 years old. I was with her to comfort her when her slightly older husband passed away five years prior. She ended up living alone in a house that was too big for one person. The maintenance was too much: cleaning, raking, taking out the trash, shoveling snow, mowing the lawn. It was too much for a single person. Initially she wanted to live there until she passed away, but on her own, it was too much to bear. She was not enjoying the quality of life she used to. The good news is that she has plenty of income and assets to do whatever she chooses.

Partly she has options because she's doing well financially. We created a nice plan for them when they were younger, and they've been consistently bringing in a steady income on their assets for over 20 years. That might not sound like much, but when you start with $2 million, a steady income could produce more than most people take home with a good full-time job. Now that she's on her own, she doesn't spend nearly as much as she brings in. At over 90 years old, she's financially ahead of where she started in retirement.

WHAT IT REALLY TAKES TO RETIRE

At some point all you have to do is tell work you're not coming in anymore and violà! You're retired. But retiring with a solid plan and simply not working anymore are two different things. When people come into my office, I offer them a portfolio analysis review. Sometimes I even do this with a room full of people at seminars. I use a program called Morningstar to analyze your portfolio, comparing your risk tolerance and risk exposure to the industry. It's a good insight into how you're investing your money. The results are sometimes shocking, and I would say that in performing this analysis thousands of times, many people who takes the test discover that they're taking on more risk than they're comfortable with and more risk than they probably need to be.

I then offer people a "Retirement Compass Report," which gives you an optional strategy for how your income can be deployed through your retirement. It analyzes your assets and shows how they may perform over your lifetime, with a little wiggle room for error and curveballs thrown in. We can use this as a general road map to see if you have enough assets to retire and that they're getting a decent rate of return. Mind you that we're not going for high risk, high reward. For retirement we're usually looking for the maximum reward for the least risk. From there I recommend guaranteed* sources of income, in addition to lower-risk growth assets. The goal is to look at the worst-case scenario and plan to do better than this, so you hopefully stay ahead of the game.

One blessing that people today are enjoying is that they can potentially be retired as long as they worked. How crazy is that? It used to be a little blip at the end of your life, and now it can be a third of your life. That's why we set up an elaborate plan that accounts for possibilities like living a long, wonderful life. If you end up leaving sooner, you pass on your extra wealth to loved ones. But if you live into your nineties, you can continue enjoying a high quality of life because the plan has provisions for payouts as long as you live.**

---

*Annuities are long-term insurance products primarily designed for retirement income. It is important to know a) that annuities and some of their features have costs associated with them like surrender charges for early withdrawals; b) that annuities used to fund IRAs do not afford any additional measure of tax deferral for the IRA owner; c) that income received from annuities and other assets may be taxable; and d) withdrawals from annuities prior to age 59 ½ may incur an additional 10% IRS tax penalty. It is important to remember that life insurance may require health underwriting and, in many instances, financial underwriting.

**Annuities are insurance products and are subject to state insurance laws and regulations. Annuities are designed to be long-term investments and may not be suitable for all investors. Annuity guarantees are based on the claims paying ability of the insurance company. Annuities can involve charges such as administrative fees, annual contract fees, rider fees, mortality & risk expense charges and surrender charges. Early withdrawals may be subject to surrender charges and can impact annuity cash values and death benefits. Withdrawing more than the guaranteed annual withdrawal amount on an annuity with an income rider can reduce the future guaranteed annual withdrawal amounts. Taxes are payable upon withdrawal of funds. An additional 10 percent IRS penalty may apply to withdrawals prior to age 59½. Annuities are not guaranteed by FDIC or any other governmental agency and are not deposits or other obligations of, or guaranteed or endorsed by any bank or savings association. When considering replacing or transferring out of an annuity it's important to understand what costs may be incurred such as surrender charges, tax consequences and the loss of death and/or income benefits.

An ethical advisor can help you prepare for any of these scenarios. They're out there waiting to help but so are the sharks. A lot of bad advisors out there are good salespeople. You want a professional to do business with, someone who's been doing this for a while, someone who is not just looking for an opportunity to make a quick buck. Retirement planning is what I do for a living, and I've been doing it 30 years. As a fiduciary I'm the kind of person you need to speak to, and this is who I am. This is not just a job or a way of making money; this is my calling and my business. Even if it's not me you end up meeting with, you can find someone with passion and dedication like me, a true fiduciary. I'll show you how in the next chapter.

11
FIND A QUALIFIED FINANCIAL SERVICES PROFESSIONAL

There's a lot of money to be made when it comes to other people's money. For some people, this represents an opportunity to be of service and genuinely helpful. A few people get into the financial industry with the promise of doing a noble thing. Others just follow the money. That's the primary reason they're there—to get as much of it for themselves as they can, no matter if it helps their clients or not.

Now I sure wish I could tell you with certainty that the good guys had deep voices and square jawlines, while the bad guys have vaudeville mustaches and heinous, cackly laughs. This is not the case. People just look like people, no matter what their intentions or motivations are. In fact some of the best salespeople who make you the biggest promises are likely also the ones to watch for.

But don't worry. There are plenty of good advisors out there for everyone. I want to ensure that you find the right person for you. In this chapter we will explore what to look for and what to be aware of when it comes to choosing an advisor. Unfortunately this is one of the biggest steps in creating a prudent retirement plan that will last longer than you do. The thing that makes it tricky is that people with vested interests might not realize they're not acting in the best interest of their clients. They might be so sold on their organization that you're banking on their own naiveite and conviction that they want to help, even if they may not be capable of truly doing so.

TIMES CHANGE

I've known advisors who started out with big ambitions, learned a lot about the best products of their times, and then continued recommending those same products decades later, because initially they were seeing great results. Times change, people change and products change with that flow. Imagine a fancy Mercedes-Benz from 1973 and a fancy Mercedes-Benz from 2023. It's an entirely different product. Today it's a computer that's also a car. Similarly retirement products have changed to fit the needs you have in this day and age. New products offer many more features that you will want throughout retirement.

Make sure your advisor keeps up to date on the latest products and has detailed conversations with you on why he or she recommends those products for you. That why is essential. A salesperson will tell you that a product is perfect for you, because it's the best. But a good advisor will show you a few products, explain what they do, and then let you make a decision about what's best for you.

Ultimately any retirement plan is just a piece of paper (or a digital document). Having the right financial advisor in your corner can help guide you to make well thought out choices when you need to act. Many people take time to go to a retirement seminar or read a book. In this book and the seminars I teach, I offer a lot of free information that people can take action on.

Unfortunately in my many years of meeting people who are getting ready to retire, I've seen that many have had a bad experience with salespeople. They're afraid to get "sold" on anything. They don't want to buy anything. You want an advisor who's not first and foremost a salesperson. Someone who can have a conversation with you. If you're unhappy in your current situation, think about this: Are you willing to improve it?

There are some great auto mechanics out there who will throw in a few freebies and make sure your car is running safe before you get back into it. But then there are some out there who will quote you a crazy price and do a lazy job of fixing it, knowing you will be back in to see them soon. It's human nature that some people out there are willing to take advantage of you to make a quick buck, and some want to help. That doesn't mean you should avoid the mechanic and do the job yourself. That could be irresponsible, dangerous and probably more costly in the long run.

Instead find a good auto mechanic and stick with them, even if you interview three or four people. Do the same with an advisor. Get out there and book a few appointments. Sit down with someone and see if they can back up their claims about how they can help you. Check their credentials. See who they're really in the business for—you or them.

A NOD TO SIMPLER TIMES

My father was born in 1940, so he grew up during the World War II era where you gave all your metal to the government, so they could make bullets, and grew war gardens in your yard, so you could be more self-sufficient. As a career policeman and outstanding dad, he was a tough guy. I gave him a new shirt one time as a gift, hoping that he might dress up and feel good about his appearance. My mom gave that same shirt back to me with the tags still on it when my dad passed a decade and a half later. He didn't wear new stuff until the old stuff was completely worn out. But he was also a happy guy, satisfied with his lot in life, with his effect on the world, with his incredibly wonderful wife, and thankfully with me, too.

It always makes me wonder why people think they need more. Sure it takes a lot of money to ensure you're going to be all set in retirement, but some people retire with tens of thousands of dollars and do okay and some people retire with millions. I often find myself worried about people with more money, because they have more choices, more expenditures, and sometimes think less about how much they're spending and can zip through their savings quickly without a clear plan.

Maybe deep down there's a crazy gold rush mentality in all of us, where we're just waiting to strike it rich. Many people at retirement age put their hopes and dreams on the next big dot-com craze, hoping they can make a fortune. But at the end of the day, true happiness comes from the little things in life, like having good friends, finding and holding onto love, and, I think, having the peace of mind that comes with not worrying about money.

If there's one thing I would wish for any retiree, it's to not feel the need to check on accounts, because they know that money is not a problem. It's just part of their plan, and the plan is already in place. They're being provide for. They can finally relax and sleep in if they want to. I strive to make sure that everyone can enjoy a peaceful retirement, because a rich quality of life is, in my opinon, better than simply being rich. Most rich people can attest that, no matter how much money you have, there's always someone out there with more.

SAFE, NOT SEXY

A salesperson might have an easier time selling you on the retirement route I like to have people consider. But here's the thing: This route benefits you and not the salesperson. The truth is that it's not some great new asset or strategy that keeps you wealthy during retirement. This strategy is simply not losing what you have. That's right! It's as simple as that. Now granted there's a lot of nuance that goes into every plan, because it should be tailored to you, but in the end, you want to slowly and cautiously grow your wealth without losing it.

Like most reputable advisors, I like diversity. I recommend lower risk products. If something will give you a guaranteed return*, I like that. It's like going to dinner and ordering steak and potatoes with a salad. It might not be that fancy new French-Asian fusion dish that costs a couple hundred dollars (the one with a tiny piece of tuna on a cracker). But those dishes can be very hit and miss.

Similarly an advisor might come along, laugh and look at your possible returns. They might have all kinds of sexy-sounding products that can bring big returns. What they may fail to disclose is that a promise of big returns can also be a possibility for big losses. Losses are not sexy. They're not what many people first consider when investing, and they're certainly not what will keep you retired for life.

---

*Annuities are long-term insurance products primarily designed for retirement income. It is important to know a) that annuities and some of their features have costs associated with them like surrender charges for early withdrawals; b) that annuities used to fund IRAs do not afford any additional measure of tax deferral for the IRA owner; c) that income received from annuities and other assets may be taxable; and d) withdrawals from annuities prior to age 59 ½ may incur an additional 10% IRS tax penalty. It is important to remember that life insurance may require health underwriting and, in many instances, financial underwriting.

Here's how you can get guaranteed returns. Some accounts are written by insurance companies that have deep pockets. They can make promises, which they guarantee through their claims paying ability, usually assisted by many smart actuaries. If they tell you that you will make a 5 percent return no matter what the market is doing, that's what you will almost certainly get.

They're 100 percent guaranteed by the insurance carrier who issues the contract. They might have a very not-sexy title, like "guaranteed fixed annuities." Many people open their eyes a little wider, because there are also some annuities out there that won't be a great fit for you or your portfolio.

But imagine getting a higher rate than you could get in a CD at the bank, with a very low risk of losing your capital. It doesn't mean you need to put your life savings there. But if you put enough of it into a guaranteed account, you know you will earn a minimum amount every month, which you can help cover your expenses. As not sexy as they are, very few people have lost so much as a nickel with fixed annuities. Keep in mind that I do not usually promote *variable* annuities, because those simply follow the market. But *fixed* annuities can have a special place in any solid retirement plan. It's something to at least strongly consider when you're deciding what's the best diversity for your portfolio.

I've had fixed index annuities provided strong returns because some these annuities will provide a credit to your account based on the performance of the underlying stock index, like the S&P 500 index for example. And when the market dropped the next year, these clients lost nothing, because the features of the fixed index annuity meant their principal was not actually invested in the market and therefore not subject to market risk. During retirement the new name of the game is not losing. Think about a guaranteed income stream that you can never outlive.

ADVISORS ARE EXPERTS

Advisors must study and get certifications to advise you. Beyond that good advisors take note of recent changes in the rules and regulations of retirement. They stay ahead of the game and make sure that your plan is always on the right path. They reach out and contact you in advance, and they are there to listen when your circumstances change and you need someone to help.

It's impossible not to get emotional about your money. That's why it's essential to have an objective advisor who isn't as intimately connected to your money help you make better decisions. For example at the end of 2020, the Patient Protection and Affordable Care Act came into play. But suddenly the Covid-19 pandemic happened, and many people were so focused on the news, they didn't hear or know anything about this act. I made sure all the people I worked with knew what this act was and how it would affect their retirement. It helped them stay up to speed and navigate the shifts.

You're a human being, not an account. Your advisor should treat you like a human being and not an account. If you were to go into the grocery store and purchase something, that relationship is transactional—you only need to get the item and be done with it. But imagine a car dealership where you will have that car for the next 20 years. That relationship should be transformational, not just transactional. You will need that car serviced and maintained. It's not just a thing you buy and then walk away from the business.

If you can find an established advisor who will be there for the next 20 to 30 years of your life, that's a great start. If they're truly there to give you guidance for making changes, marriages, births, deaths, divorces and affect your legacy planning, then you've found the right person.

I have daughters who are 12 and 15 years old. I will be in this business 20 years from now, helping people through retirement, because I'm modeling a good work ethic for them by showing them it's good to be of service to the world.

HOW TO FIND THE RIGHT ADVISOR

Talk to your friends, get referrals, sit down and interview professionals. See if you connect and are speaking the same language. Some advisors may not be a good fit or suited for your personality, kind of like finding a general practitioner. You want a doc who is looking out for you and who you connect with. Speak with your advisor to see how they communicate, if they can explain difficult concepts clearly, and if they're aligned with your vision. See if they answer their phone. Many people pay lip service, but I'm on my cell phone and give out my number to clients. I should be on speed dial for my clients if they need me.

One time had a sweet older lady come up to me after one of my seminars. She said she was suspicious of me, but she liked my personality. She set up an appointment and met with me, then she decided that she did indeed trust me and wanted me to help her with her portfolio. I was delighted at the opportunity to connect with someone and be of genuine service. I'm more about creating a real relationship and helping people understand why certain retirement strategies meet their needs. I want to be there as a real person who listens to and helps them when they're struggling.

FIND AN ADVISOR WITHOUT AN AGENDA

Last and probably most importantly, you want an advisor who is there to help you find the best products that work for your portfolio, not just random products they're paid to sell. Look for designations that make you more aware of this.

For starters some advisors working for a big company may get compensated extra by selling those company products. In fact they may even have deadlines and quotas for how much of those products to sell, even if it's not a good product for the person they're selling it to. Make sure that any company you go to is a registered investment advisor (RIA). This means they're legally obligated to put the needs of their clients first, think about what your needs are, and disclose any conflicts of interest. Sadly without this tag, they can sell you anything they think is suitable for you.

Of course most people have to earn a living, and there's nothing wrong with that. But I don't make money off of people, I make money by helping people. My first priority is to put people in a better situation, and from that, I get a small percentage. Some people have a distaste for financial advisors, because they think they're there for the money. Which is sometimes true. But we don't fault a doctor for making money when they heal you—they paid for 10 expensive years of medical school and owe big money for that education. An advisor who puts your needs first and helps you choose the best products and services for your retirement plan is doing a great job in securing your financial future, and they earn their keep year after year, making sure that your needs are met and that your retirement portfolio is doing well.

What I've found works best in my own practice is that I disclose my fees and what I'm making to people. I have no agenda. I don't set commission rates. I only sell people assets that will work for them. This earns me trust, long-term relationships and plenty of referrals from satisfied people who are better off financially. Think about the last time you experienced exceptional service for a doctor or a mechanic. Didn't you want to tell your friends and family about that person?

A referral is an honor to get, because someone that I've helped out and done business with will put their neck on the line and risk their reputation by offering me as an advisor. I appreciate that someone trusts me enough to pass on my info to a friend or family member. This is very powerful and rewarding for me. It's a big complement and a thank you. From the day someone entrusts their money with me, that's a big step, and I never forget that. I go out of my way to protect each of my clients. I work for the people I serve and not the companies. I will take a stand with the people and not with the companies.

I have one client in particular up in North Jersey, who I helped with their portfolio. That person has since passed away, but before this happened, that person referred children, family members, neighbors and friends to me. Knowing I had that much impact on a life and gave that much satisfaction regarding my work is an honor and a blessing, and I do not take it for granted. It's very rewarding to know I can be of service to clients' legacies and their networks of people.

12
WHAT'S NEXT?

If you were to get a baseball cap to shade your face on a sunny day, you might think that a one-size-fits-all cap is good enough. It's not made for your head size or your length (or lack) of hair, but it still blocks out the sun, despite being uncomfortable. It's not a big deal, because it's only $20, and you can always pick up another if you find something better.

For anyone whose tried on a hat that fits them just right, you can't go back to a one-size-fits-all hat. Or a one-size-fits-all anything for that matter.

Imagine spending 10, 20 or even over 30 years on a one-size-fits-all retirement plan. Who would possibly want to be uncomfortable throughout retirement, because they went with a basic plan that didn't accommodate their needs? That's why I tell people that your retirement plan should be as unique as your fingerprints. It's got to be designed specifically for you and your needs, for the needs of your family, and for allowing the flexibility to deal with your unique challenges that you will need to overcome. Everyone wants a safe retirement portfolio that lasts longer than they do, but that means different assets and options for different people.

Imagine a 63-year-old single man with no kids who loves to stay at home and watch television, compared to a couple who retires at 70 years old, loves traveling, has three children and fourteen grandchildren. Those are just the broad brush strokes, because we haven't even looked at what their jobs were before retirement, how much they want to spend during retirement, what their health and fitness levels are like, what foods they enjoy eating, whether they like to go out to restaurants or stay home and cook, whether they own their home, and hundreds of other factors that influence what you need for retirement and where to invest it.

This chapter is designed to show you how to take everything that you learned in this book and make use of it. After all good advice isn't good if you don't act on it. The only thing worse than being ignorant is kicking yourself, because you knew better and didn't do anything to change your life.

MAKE GOOD CHOICES

The right asset allocation and risk can be as important as the actual dollar amount you've saved for retirement. You've already made the good choice of saving money for retirement, so now you can continue to make good choices and tuck it away in the right place until you need to spend it. Proper asset allocation is much more than just taking money from one pocket and putting it into the other, it can actually save you from market crashes, recessions, offer guaranteed income and save big on taxes.

Working with a professional financial advisor is a good choice, especially if you can get comprehensive support across all of your

assets. You have more than just money to consider; you should also be aware that your retirement portfolio includes your:
- Insurance planning
- Beneficiary review
- Retirement planning
- Financial needs analysis
- Analysis of present and future expenses
- Estate preservation
- Income planning

It's typically the analysis and planning part that most people don't prefer to look at or do themselves. Yet without this essential pillar that supports the foundation of your retirement portfolio, you could be setting yourself up for massive risk and possible financial failure. In my experience people's needs are best fulfilled by focusing on processes and, most importantly, their individual needs.

Additionally asset allocation isn't just a one-and-done thing at retirement. Your needs change. Markets change. Where you store and draw money from may change throughout retirement. Having someone you trust that you can come back to can make a world of difference.

SOLVE PROBLEMS BEFORE THEY HAPPEN

The best time to deal with a problem is before it happens. No matter what you think may happen during retirement, the unexpected always finds a way to surprise you—you just don't know when or what it will be. In every retirement portfolio that I've helped build, there are multiple different scenarios that I try to anticipate, just in case. I've also been proud of my partnership with my clients and enjoy seeing them succeed in retirement. This is not to brag but I believe if you start thinking about retirement early and yes, work with an advisor, you will be further ahead when you decide the time is right to retire. It's to point out that these plans succeed for a specific reason.

Knowing what you have and how much to spend is a great start to continued success. It lets you comfortably draw down certain assets, meet your income needs, and know you're okay financially. Beyond that you can also allocate assets in safe places so that no matter what, you're guaranteed to be stable financially. Nobody predicted the world closing down for two years during the Covid-19 pandemic. But people who realized that a disaster could strike at any moment were prepared to swerve their portfolios and stay above water. Others who weren't prepared and faced financial difficulties.

Once you're aware of the possible scenarios you may face in retirement, you're more prepared to plan for them and solve the problems well in advance. That's what I try to guide people toward so that they can experience smooth sailing throughout their retirement, no matter how choppy the waters get.

TAKE ACTION

Once you've identified what it is you want your retirement plan to look like and you're ready to do something about it, the next step is to take action. Most people don't know enough about the nuances, rules and regulations of retirement planning that they can confidently and competently navigate all these challenges and come out ahead. They may only save a few dollars in the end by not hiring a professional to help them. In fact it could cost money in lost earnings, missed savings, down-market turns and last-minute surprises that end up costing more than they believed they were saving.

Here's the truth of the matter: When I go for sushi, I like an expert to get me fresh fish sliced perfectly so that I enjoy the experience and don't get sick. When I get my oil changed, the experts do it in fifteen minutes and don't leave my garage a hot mess with oil stains everywhere. When I need an electrician, I call an expert, because it's not worth me shocking and killing myself to save a few bucks.

There are some things you can fix by reading a book or watching a video, but your retirement plan should not be one of them. *Can you do your own retirement planning?* Sure but perhaps not well. Why chance it if there is the potential for a big failure?

On the other hand, it's surprisingly easy to find a good financial advisor once you know what to look for, which you do now. Call me old school, but I like to set up a face-to-face meeting, so I can shake your hand, look you in the eyes, and listen to what you're hoping to get out of your retirement. I do that so I can offer my honest advice. If you decide to enter into a fiduciary contract with me, I always take your side and help you make informed decisions that help you stick to your plan and manage your assets.

If I'm not the right planner for you, you're welcome to use any information, and we can shake hands again and part as friends. The reason I offer zero pressure meetings is because I'm an advisor, not a salesperson. There is a big difference between the two. If someone is pressuring you to buy into something, they're a salesperson. When it comes to your retirement plan, your advisor should let you know what works best for you, educate you and then offer you the option to make your own informed choices.

BOOK A MEETING

I am confident that I can be of service as a retirement planner to people who walk in my door for a meeting. If your retirement plan is well thought out and you have plenty of diversified assets, I will tell you point blank that you do not need a financial advisor; although, you are, of course, always welcome to use my services if and when you do need my help to make hard decisions or to keep you up to date on changes in policies, rules and regulations.

Here's what you will get out of a 45-minute meeting:
- A thorough evaluation of your portfolio and assets.
- Targeted questions based on what you have that can help you build a stronger portfolio.
- A clear path for how you can reach your financial goals in retirement and where to go next.

People enjoy my financial services for a number of reasons. I would like to say it's because I'm a nice guy with honest intentions, but I suspect these are the main reasons they stick around for the long haul:

1. **I listen.** It's your retirement plan, and I'm here to help you, not the other way around. Your plan needs to work for you and your family, and I'm only here to help you make the best choices for you. Listening, actually hearing you and asking follow-up questions is the first step to understanding what your needs are. I will take an objective and honest look at your assets and tell you how you could fund the lifestyle you prefer.

2. **I'm proactive.** I work hard on your plan to make sure that you understand everything and that your plan itself has a number of strategies for dealing with surprises. I set you up to win so that your assets are protected, and if all goes well, you will also get a nice windfall. I leverage my 30-plus years of experience to help you make better financial decisions. Many of my clients retire with more money than they thought they would ever have, which is always a good surprise.

3. **I'm available.** I get that life has surprises here and there for everyone. That's why I pick up the phone, even when I'm on vacation. It's so that I can help you work through whatever it is you're dealing with. Now, fortunately, this is

a rare occasion, because most of the time will be smooth sailing (otherwise my wife and daughters would get mad at me for picking up the phone). In over 30 years of working in this field, I know that sometimes you just need to hear a voice on the other end of the phone who is listening to you and letting you know that everything will be okay, especially when I have expert knowledge for how and why everything will be okay.

It's important for me to check in quarterly or more often to touch base and visit with you. Most of the time, it's just nice to say hi, but we can always deal with anything that's going on and make changes, if needed. Even clients who move away still keep in touch, and we still talk about their retirement, how I can help them, and what they need. It's also important for me to be available in the way that works best for you, be it in person, on the phone, via a text message or even through an email.

I like to keep up to date on everything that's going on, not just the bad. When you're retired, there are births and deaths, grandkid events, kids moving out and kids moving back in. It's nice to hear how things are going in general, but all those changes also have an effect on you and your retirement plan.

I also keep an open line of communication so that you can keep yourself up to date on anything that you're interested in and always have access to me if you need it. On my website I have all sorts of updated information to keep you in the know. I have an email campaign that sends you links to useful articles and notifies you of any upcoming changes in retirement planning as they happen, such as tax law changes or other important topics that may affect you.

Communication is important, because life changes over time. Nobody goes from point A to point B in a straight line. There are always unique situations that change your life, some for the better, like weddings and grandchildren, and some more challenging, like unexpected home repairs or needing a new car.

Communication is simply a part of honest caring, which is what I've focused on providing for every client for the last 30-plus years. It's the biggest difference between any financial services professional, because you can get the latest technology and sign up for the top training, but at the end of the day, if you don't actually care about the people you work with, you won't do what's best for them. The best thing is that there are some advisors out there who can get you all the above: The personal touch and care mixed with the latest technology and top training.

For me there's no magic formula. I just show up to work every day to do what I'm passionate about, which is helping you and your family build and maintain retirement plans that offer you the most personalized, diverse, hassle-free and risk appropriate assets that will keep you financially healthy and happy. That's it. For anyone looking for a shortcut, I can honestly say that some things in life are best served without shortcuts. You would know that's true if you've ever had a buttery croissant made over three days at a real French bakery versus a bland supermarket croissant made the same day.

To be honest, nothing in life is that simple, and retirement planning is no different. We're talking about the next 20 to 30 years of your life, God willing. I've had conversations with clients where one spouse wants to move south and enjoy the sunshine during retirement, while the other wants to stay closer to grandchildren. It happens, even with the most compatible of couples. The key is to get on the same page about what resources are available, what kind of monthly income that can lead to, and how much you can leave behind. Your retirement plan is more than a few simple decisions. It should be professionally mapped out and a perfect fit for you.

If you think about it this way, a doctor may order a blood test to get specific information about your body. Then they can diagnose and treat you. In the same way, it's my job to run various tests that can help you understand everything you need to know about your finances and how those will fit into your overall goals. You may be a marathon runner who eats organic salads every day, and your neighbor may prefer watching television and smoking cigarettes. No judgment, but you may have different health care concerns.

THANK YOU

I want to sincerely thank you for taking the time to read this book. It's a part of my legacy that I'm able to offer honest advice to good people, and I want you to live a long and fruitful retirement. I know there may have been some complex sections of this book, so if you ever need anything cleared up, please reach out to me, and I will get back to you.

Here's to a thriving, long and joyous retirement. I'm sending you and the people you love my regards.

– Carl

ABOUT THE AUTHOR

CARL FELDMAN, PRESIDENT OF FELDMAN FINANCIAL SERVICES, LLC

Dedication, hard work and an honest approach to serving the needs of clients in the New Jersey Shore area are overriding values that Carl focused on when he started his financial services career in 1991. He has built his business using a philosophy geared toward helping people achieve their retirement dreams.

Carl knows there is no substitute for knowledge when answering these common client questions: "When will I have enough to retire, and will it last for the rest of my life?" His familiarity of retirement products is superior, and he shares the information in a comfortable, friendly and casual manner clients truly appreciate. He recognizes that retirement decisions may not necessarily be simple or straightforward, which is why he is dedicated to earning his clients' trust by providing them with advantages other financial professionals can't.

Carl earned his Master of Business Administration degree from Wagner College and is a lifelong New Jersey resident. For fun, Carl coaches softball in his local community and enjoys fishing, boating and spending time with his wife and daughters.

Made in the USA
Middletown, DE
15 October 2023